The Booktalker's Bible

The Booktalker's Bible

How to Talk About the Books You Love to Any Audience

Chapple Langemack

2003
LIBRARIES UNLIMITED
A Division of Greenwood Publishing Group, Inc.
Westport, CT 06881

LIBRARIES UNLIMITED
A Division of Greenwood Publishing Group, Inc.
88 Post Road West
Westport, CT 06881
1-800-225-5800
www.lu.com

Library of Congress Cataloging-in-Publication Data

ISBN 1-56308-944-0

*For Will, of course, whose love,
support and willingness to hide
in the basement never wavered
(Hey, you can come out now!).*

*And for my booktalking colleagues
whose prowess and generosity
never fail to inspire.*

Contents

Acknowledgments

My heartfelt thanks to the following booktalkers and other "pros from Dover" who shared their experiences and expertise:

Angelina Benedetti
Darcy Brixey
Sharon Chastain
Peg Dombek
Kirsten Edwards
Rayna Holtz
Mary Huebscher
Chance Hunt
Tom Joselyn
Holly Koelling
Teri S. Lesesne
Jeani Littrell-Kwik

Georgia Lomax
Sharon Macdonald
Judy T. Nelson
Elizabeth Panni
Tom Reynolds
Dawn Rutherford
Karlan Sick
Sandra Smith
Aarene Storms
Kathy Svajdlenka
Roz Thompson
JoAnn VanderKooi

Preface

Ah, booktalking! The thrill of being able to escape from your normal workplace and speak engagingly to an appreciative group about books you truly enjoy, bringing your audience to a fever pitch of anticipation and book lust. Oh, the accolades, the satisfaction of sharing.

Ah, booktalking! The terror of facing a group of strangers and recognizing the possibility that no sensible words may come out of your mouth. Plots, characters, and titles may totally escape you. Oh, the fear, the sense of foolishness. Whoever thought this was a good idea?

Occasional moments of panic and terror aside, booktalking *is* a good idea. As a matter of fact, it's a terrific idea. How better to generate enthusiasm for books and the whole concept of the pleasure that reading can bring than to tell a group of people about books you love?

Booktalking is, quite simply, talking about books. It requires you, a great book, and an audience. That's all. You, clever soul that you are, have read the book and extracted its essence so that you can present it to your audience in a concise, entertaining way. The point is not to tell everything about the book, but the flavor of it, a snapshot if you will, to tantalize your audience into taking their own journey into that book.

The other great thing about booktalking (besides the simple fact that you are promoting books you love) is that there is no single "right" way to do it. There are as many different styles of booktalks as there are booktalkers. Quiet, intense, dramatic, or flamboyant—everyone has a different technique. Certainly presentation skills are involved in booktalking, but it's not so much a performance as a connection. It's about you sharing with your audience. All you have to do is find a way to talk that is comfortable for you and interesting for your audience.

Like any new skill, the way to learn it is to do it. I'll give you a way to structure, plan, and present your booktalks. And I'll throw in some sample booktalks—both mine and some of my booktalking pals—to give you an idea of what it's all about. Then it's your turn to go out and do it. You might be a little nervous your first time out, but that will quickly pass. Once you start focusing on the books you love, you'll have a great time—and so will your audience.

Why Booktalk?

I'll give you that I'm biased in a big way, but I think a better question is why *not* booktalk? If you are trying to generate enthusiasm for books and reading, then booktalking is a grand way to do it. Booktalking creates a personal connection with any audience, and it needs no specialized equipment. You can adapt and change a booktalk at a moment's notice; the only cost is your time and preparation—nearly anyone can do it. What's not to like?

Okay, okay. As terrific as I think booktalking is, you need to think about why, in your particular situation, you would want to start a booktalking program. Booktalking is a public presentation, albeit a somewhat specialized one. As with any public presentation, whether it is on your home turf or out in the community, you first have to determine what it is you're trying to accomplish. This is important for your own planning purposes as well as for making a case for booktalking to your administration.

So why should you be booktalking? Maybe your library is the best-kept secret in town, and you want everyone in the community to know that you're there. Maybe you're a school librarian who wants to make your teachers aware that there are new titles out there, and they needn't cling to their twenty-year-old reading lists. Maybe you want to highlight new books in your collection. Maybe you don't have many new books in your collection, and you want to entice folks with the oldies but goldies that you do have. Maybe you just want people to know that the library is still focused on books and reading. Your purpose will determine your message, and your message will determine what audiences you seek and which books you choose to talk about.

There are three standard questions that professional communicators ask themselves when doing any kind of presentation—be it a presidential speech or an advertisement for cat food. It behooves a booktalker to consider the same questions.

1. Who Is My Audience?

You've thought about your purpose for booktalking. That should give you some idea as to who your audience is. If you are using booktalks to cloak information about a library political issue or fundraising campaign, then you'll want to target adults of voting age in your political district. If you want to raise the library's visibility among the adult population at large, then you'll want to target community groups of all stripes. Do you want to bring teens into the library—or at least let them know that they're welcome and that the library has something for them? That's when you go to where teens are—the schools. Speaking of schools, do you wish you, as a public librarian, had better communication with the teachers in your district? Maybe booktalking to the faculty could help start that process.

The great thing about booktalking is that it works for nearly any audience. School librarians can talk about new titles they want their students to be aware of or titles on a subject recently assigned. Public librarians serving children and young adults find booktalking is often their entrée into a school, whether it's booktalking to elementary students around the upcoming summer reading program or firing up middle school students to participate in a young reader's choice award. Have you ever considered booktalking classics to high school students? It can be done—and quite successfully, too.

But booktalking doesn't stop there. Think about the many service and professional organizations in your community. Rotary, Kiwanis, Lions Club, American Association of University Women, and business and professional women's organizations all must mine the community for speakers for their meetings. They may not know it yet, but a lively, well-crafted booktalk is just what they need for their program, and their meetings are just the venue you need to spread the word about books—and about your library or organization. Retirement home activity directors will welcome you and your booktalk with open arms. Often book clubs and other literary activities are already going on in retirement homes, and these are the perfect tie-in. Speaking of book clubs, how many of them are there in your community? Don't you think they'd be glad of a friendly face from the library and some fresh ideas for discussion books?

But you don't always need to leave home to booktalk or reach an audience. Many libraries have begun sponsoring mother–daughter or father–son book groups. How does such a group get started on the road to reading? Booktalks. Why not talk to parents and kids in your community about books they'd enjoy reading aloud as a family?

2. What Message Do I Want to Convey?

This is the next big question to ask yourself. Again, it will depend on your basic purpose. When I booktalk around the county, I always want to send the message that the library is a vital, lively place where reading and books get first priority. I want folks to think of the library as the best, most expert resource in town when they're looking for something to read.

The other message I most want to convey is that reading is a legitimate and enjoyable activity. That may sound patently obvious or even just plain goofy, but it's surprisingly necessary. Adults in our breakneck-paced society have to make choices about how to spend their precious time. It's too often duty first, pleasure later. How many times have you heard someone say—or said yourself—"I just don't have time to read"? Adults often need a subtle pep talk on the pleasures of reading—how it can stir the imagination and soothe the soul. They often need permission to indulge in that pleasure. They need reassurance that it's a right and noble thing to do and that it's okay to let something else go for a while so they can read. Bless Oprah Winfrey and her book club—she sanctioned reading like no one else, giving it a real weight in people's lives. It's telling that since Oprah gave up the book club business, everyone from the *National Geographic* to talk-show host Kelly Ripa have jumped on the bandwagon. I'm happy to chime right in there and reinforce the message as well. If I'm part of a merry throng, or even a movement for reading, then so much the better.

Pleasure is what I emphasize. I often startle an audience by giving them not only verbal but written permission to quit reading a book they're not enjoying. I give my audiences a "Get Out of This Book Free" pass to use on any book they choose. They almost unfailingly giggle nervously and then ask for extra passes. "My friend needs one of these, too!" is a common comment. Of course, I include a booklist on the other side so they'll have something else to try.

Get Out of This Book Guilt Free

You've tried and tried, you've gone along thinking it will get better, thinking you should like this book, but you just don't. Here's a secret: if you're not enjoying it, you don't have to finish it. Use this special dispensation to put the book down. Try another listed on the other side of this pass, and see if you don't like it better.

This pleasure message is nonverbal as well. When I weave stories from books around an audience, they are captured by the tale itself—but also by my enthusiasm. If I can derive such enjoyment from books, why can't they? I had an older woman in a retirement home approach me after a booktalk and say, "You know, I've never been a reader, but you make me think I might want to try it." Hurrah! If she does or if she doesn't, she got the message I was trying to convey.

3. What Action Do I Want the Audience to Take?

When you are done with your presentation, what is it you want your audience to do? Do you want them to rush up and pluck the books you talked about from your hands? Do you want them to head into the library the next time they want something to read? Maybe you want them to think more seriously about reading as a leisure activity. Do you want them to go home and tell their family and their neighbors that the library certainly seems like a lively, useful place, worthy of support? Perhaps you want them to think and say that the library is the institution in town that is most devoted to the cause of books and reading.

Although I'd be glad if every member of every group I talked to rushed to the phone, the computer or their local library to request the titles I presented (and sometimes, praise be, that happens), I really have two basic goals. I want my audience to "remember" reading as an activity in their life, and I want to soften the ground for them to contact the library. And I hope I've given them motivation with the enticing titles I've presented. I've also established a personal connection. They now know someone from the library, and it might not now be such a stretch to stop in.

Then I give them the tools for that second step. I tell them where their closest library is. I give them the toll-free phone number for the central Answer Line that can take their requests. I tell them about our Web site and where to look on it for more reading recommendations. I tell them about the fabulous authors that will be speaking at the library. If I could, I'd issue library cards on the spot. Maybe you can. It's a great idea.

Think about what your own goals are for booktalking. You may have several, and it may vary from audience to audience. Then build your philosophical foundation—plan who your audiences will be, what your message will be, and how you want them to react. That's the first step in building a great booktalking program.

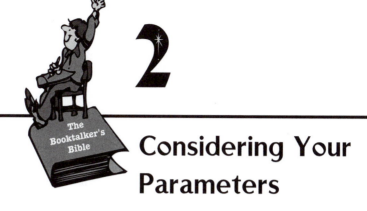

2

Considering Your Parameters

So you've taken some time to think about your purpose, your message, and your audience. Now take just a little more time before you start tracking down your audience to think about the parameters of your program. Decide ahead of time what you will and won't do. You may start out thinking you'll booktalk to anyone, any place, any time, but my guess is you'll revise that after some time goes by. It is truly much easier to give this some serious thought beforehand and begin in the way that you intend to go on than to explain later why you're not doing "that" anymore, whatever "that" happens to be. Give the following issues some consideration.

Size of Group

Must the group be of a certain size? I've booktalked to groups of five or six before, and it can be a great experience, but you need to decide if it suits your purpose and time constraints. Is it truly worth your while to travel to meet with a small group? Consider, too, that the mood and dynamic is considerably different with a very small (or very large) group. A small group will be by nature much more conversational and prone to interruption than a larger group. Large groups have their own challenges. Are you up for booktalking to a school auditorium full of seventh graders? I think that goes beyond booktalking and into performance art, but it's for you to decide what you are comfortable trying. Decide in advance the minimum and maximum size of group you will consider.

Age of Group

If you are looking at booktalking in a school situation, you'll need to decide with which ages you are comfortable. If you're up for all grades, that's terrific, but realize that you must prepare differently for each age group; the booktalks you'll do for sixth graders are not what's appropriate or effective for third graders. The variety of ages that you include on a single day's booktalking venture will have an impact on your preparation time and the number of books and amount of support material you must lug with you.

Geography

How far will you travel to give a booktalk? Will your library or agency reimburse you for mileage, or will the group? Will you speak strictly within your service area? What will you do if a neighboring library hears of your prowess and wants you to be a guest speaker? Think these things out now and discuss them with your supervisor.

My own geographic parameters are that I will travel anywhere in the county, which is our service area. I will travel to a neighboring county if at least half the members of the group are residents of our service area. It's not uncommon for a group to meet just over the county line, but draw its membership from both counties. I will go as a guest speaker to other libraries (if I'm asked!) two or three times a year at no charge to them. That's what my supervisor and I have agreed upon as a reasonable number. It's enough to be a good neighbor but not enough to siphon large amounts of my time away from our own service population.

Time

I'm going to assume that you are booktalking while on the clock for your library, school, or agency. Are you willing to go to those early breakfast meetings that some service organizations are so fond of? Can you be sensible, let alone entertaining, at 7 A.M.? Can your schedule flex to absorb those hours? What about evening hours? If you are a public librarian, you probably are already working a couple of nights. Will you accept engagements in addition to your regular evening shift or instead of it? How will your shift get covered if the latter is the case? These same issues arise with weekends. In general, none of us want to work any more weekends than we have to, but that's when many groups gather. What will you do if someone asks you to do a Saturday booktalk? Think about it and consult with your supervisor, your significant other, and your pet. Your decision will have an impact on all of them.

Speaking of time, you also need to take your preparation time into consideration. When you are flawlessly performing a booktalk, it certainly looks as if it's the combination of natural gifts and the inspiration of the moment, but in reality there's a lot of work and preparation behind that fabulous three-minute talk. You need time to read—and read a wide assortment of books because not every book you pick up is going to be a prime booktalking candidate. You need time to think about and to prepare your booktalk. And you need time to practice your presentation. It's the rare employer who will underwrite all of these activities so give some thought to just how much time you'll need and then have a discussion with your supervisor as to what might be accomplished on work time.

Money

One of the first questions you'll be asked is what you charge. I'm assuming that if you're doing this on your employer's nickel, then you cannot ethically accept money for yourself. Perhaps your library or agency requires a token reimbursement for your time or mileage. Maybe there is a fee only for speaking engagements out of your service area. If money must change hands, be clear about how much and under what circumstances. I was tickled by a story told by Evelyn Oppenheimer, one of the pioneers of oral book reviewing, which was so popular in the 1940s and 1950s. She recounted having to travel by train to get to one engagement in Texas, sharing the car not only with other passengers but a two-week-old calf that was crying for its mother. In such a case, she dryly advised, one should expand the expense account to cover a little something to steady the nerves.

Again, think carefully about your message here. If you are booktalking as a public relations tool, then charging a fee might not set the tone you're after. Or your board may feel that charging sets a tone of fiscal responsibility. Whatever policy is put in place, decide in advance how you'll handle this issue.

Frequency

Once a group has heard you, they'll no doubt be delighted and want you to come back again and again, which is quite a gratifying predicament to be in. I find this to be particularly true with retirement homes. Activity directors are often grateful for a free program that they can schedule on a recurring basis. As much fun as an older audience is, and as glad as I am to talk to them, I find that after a number of programs I'm no longer fresh for a repeat group, my repertoire is exhausted, and my schedule doesn't have room for anything else. Think about your limits in this regard before you agree to that monthly book chat. Twice-a-year visits work best for me, and quarterly visits are really the most I can do for groups who are keen on having me back on a recurring basis. It's enough time to refresh my repertoire and still make the visit a special occasion.

Also think about what you'll say to the Group from Hell should they ask you back. You know, the ones that are combative, inattentive, or just plain distracted. Setting your booktalking parameters is like having a collection development policy for the materials you purchase. You have guidance for accepting and declining invitations.

Booktalking is like baseball, a day on the reference desk, or life, for that matter. Some engagements go spectacularly well, and some just never catch fire. It might be something going on with the group; it might be something going on with you.

I still remember a booktalk I gave for a group of women at a retirement community early on in my present job. I could tell throughout my booktalk that somehow I just wasn't clicking. I was never able to make a real connection, and I felt it. I don't know if it was my presentation style, my choice of books, or if these ladies were just in a collective bad mood. At the end of my presentation, I knew that despite the polite response (or maybe because of it) that this group would not invite me back—and so far I've been right.

The truth is, you win some and you lose some. The great thing is, you don't lose very many. Bombs are few and far between, especially with adult audiences. After all, they've made the effort to invite you, and they've come because they are interested in your topic. They have a vested interest in your success. Think of the figure-skating audiences who applaud to buck up a faltering ice skater. They really are on your side.

The other great thing is that when the rare disaster strikes, the feeling of dissatisfaction is often mutual, and you won't have to worry about accepting or declining a second invitation. But in case you do, make sure you have your guidelines in place.

Schedule

And while we're talking about your time and fitting groups in your schedule, think about how many booktalks you realistically think you can do before you launch your program. Four booktalks a month sounds benign before you realize that that's one a week—in addition to everything else you do. Taking into consideration preparation and travel time, can you realistically do it? Maybe you'll want to start small and build your program as your repertoire and confidence increases. Give it some thought *before* you start taking those phone calls.

Also make sure your calendar gives you a true picture of your activities and commitments so that you don't inadvertently make a date to booktalk during a week when you really need to be preparing next year's budget or writing your monthly report. Trying to prepare for a booktalk concurrently with another major project is stress you don't need, so make sure the prep time that you need for big projects (including your booktalks) are noted on your calendar.

If your library is anything like mine, you don't want to schedule yourself out of the building on the day after a holiday, or after any closed day for that matter. It was always a madhouse in the branch on those days—trying to fit in two days of work while dealing with twice the normal number of patrons. Is that clear day on your calendar your first day back from vacation? That's a bad day to booktalk. Even if you're super organized and have your books ready to go before you leave, booktalking is not what you'll want to turn your attention to the minute you return to work. Give yourself a reentry day.

I once took several days off just before a booktalking engagement. Then I compounded my error by misreading my calendar and putting a voice message on my phone with an incorrect date of return. My poor contact called me to confirm my appearance and got my voicemail cordially telling her I wouldn't be at work on the day of her scheduled booktalk. I just about gave the poor woman a heart attack, not to mention cauliflower ear from phoning everyone in the library system trying to figure out where I was and what I was really doing. Talk about life's embarrassing moments. Now I'm much more careful about my schedule—and about confirming my appearances.

If you take the time to think about what you can and can't do before you start promoting your booktalking program, you'll save yourself a lot of grief, not to mention pregnant pauses on the phone while you try to figure out an answer to an issue you hadn't anticipated.

Getting Booked

So you've thought about your purpose, your message, your audience, and your parameters. It's time to go out and get your audience. Whether you plan to do a series of on-site booktalks or go out to community groups you need to get the word out. I visualize publicity as a series of rings, like a target or a stone thrown in water. You're the bull's eye (or the rock). Start with yourself and work your way out. So what's your first step?

Tell Everyone You Know

This is one step you definitely don't need to keep within the confines of your library, school, or agency. Mention your booktalking program to everyone from your friends and neighbors to your dentist. Why make small talk about the weather when you can chat about your booktalks? Put your fear of megalomania aside. It's interesting—really. And it's not like it's the *only* thing you're going to talk about. Become a little obsessed when you're first starting out. That's how all great things start, yes? I once heard the comedian Steve Martin say that it wasn't talent but focus and a little obsession that made him successful.

Here's a case in point. I talked to my friend Nikki about booktalking and how much I enjoyed it and that I was looking for more visibility and new audiences. So when Nikki was talking to a local bookstore owner, she felt free to recommend me as a program. Voila. Another gig. I suspect the bookstore owner paid more attention to Nikki, a friend and customer, than she would have paid to me had I been promoting myself.

I know this smacks of that terrible '80s word "networking," but the fact is, it's effective and can lead to all kinds of serendipitous places. Everyone's first reaction is to help, just let him or her know what you want. It's as simple as "I'm looking for new audiences for my booktalks. Do you know

13

of any group that might be interested?" Need I say that you must have business cards on you at all times for this to be effective?

Tell Your Staff

We often get so involved in our own responsibilities and projects at work that we forget that everyone else on staff doesn't always know what we're doing. Make sure that your library, school, or agency staff knows about your booktalking program. Prepare an easily repeatable sound bite—you know, the one you developed by telling everyone else you know—and tell everyone. Tell them individually: "Oh, Debbie. We've just started this booktalking program and I'm very excited about it." Tell them in staff meetings: "I just wanted you all to be aware that we've begun this booktalking program, and I think it will be something really fun to offer to our patrons." Put a note on the staff bulletin board. Run a recurring notice in the staff memo. Probably the most effective thing you can do to make staff aware is a booktalking demonstration. Get yourself on the agenda of the staff meeting and take ten minutes to do a booktalk. Then the staff will really know what you're talking about.

The smartest thing I ever did was ask for ten minutes on the agenda of our central staff orientation. In other words, I get a whack at every new staff member we hire, from librarians to computer technicians to shipment drivers. I give them a brief overview of my job, booktalk for a few minutes, and ask them to refer patrons interested in a speaker to me. I give them a list of the books I have talked to them about (as you'll discover later, it's a Golden Rule!) with my name and contact information on it. I figure they'll tuck that in their orientation notebook, and it will be retrievable when they need it.

I love the fact that this includes everyone hired in our system and not just public service staff. Now when I need a special favor from Terry in shipping, he has a much better idea what I'm up to. He's helping me accomplish something with which he is familiar, rather than just coping with yet another demand on his time.

Persistence is the best advice I can give you on this front. The bigger your agency, the more people to tell, the more turnover, so keep putting the message out there. When I managed a branch library, we were always so busy and there was always so much information coming in from so many sources that I developed an information filter. I really had to hear about or read about something several times for it to register. So don't put a single message out somewhere and think you've done it. Why do you think the same commercial airs over and over again? Advertisers know they don't have your full attention. They know you're just as likely to be talking with your kids or making a sandwich when their message comes on, so they tell you again. And again. And again. Remember that classic old educational theory: Tell them what you're going to tell them, tell them, and tell them what you told them. It can't hurt. This came home to me again recently as I was giving a presentation to some of our branch staff on a topic that I thought had been done to death. Not only was it not old news or patently obvious as I had thought, the information was a revelation to many staff members. So take it from me, you really can't repeat yourself too often.

While you're at it, vary the medium of your message. My mother-in-law managed an antique shop for many years. She knew that customers saw new things when she moved the merchandise around. Moving a vase from a low shelf to a table top invariably prompted regular customers to remark, "Oh, is that new?" So move your message around, put it in the staff memo for a few weeks, then put up a notice on the bulletin board for a few weeks, or put a note in everyone's inbox. It all depends on the size of your staff and what vehicles of communication you have to work with. Put tent cards on the tables in the lunchroom. Send valentines. Bring cookies or muffins one day with a "these cookies are sponsored by" message attached. One of the most effective communication methods in our building is notices on the bathroom doors (not the stalls, but the entry door), but I leave it to you as to whether that's effective or intrusive. Use your imagination, go forth, and spread the word.

While you're spreading your message to your fellow staff members, don't forget to tell them what you want them to do. Remember that third question in building presentations: What action do you want your audience to take? Tell them, "I hope you'll tell our patrons about this new program." Or "Please let me know of any groups you know of that might be interested."

Post Your Premises

So your staff knows what you're doing, everyone you've ever met knows what you're doing. It's time to let your clientele know what's up. Before you start printing notices or posters, take a tour of your facility. Go out to the parking lot and come in through the front door (and how long has it been since you been in the front door?). Make note of all the places that can catch a patron's eye. Don't limit yourself to the bulletin board that is probably in the lobby of the building. Is there a long walk to the entrance of the building? How about a series of Burma Shave style signs along the entry? Wander around the building. Where do patrons tend to congregate or spend the most time? Again, perhaps tent cards on the study tables. Create a large supply and replace them frequently. Note "please take this card for future reference" on the cards. If not on the study tables, then how about in the stacks? Post notices on the end of the fiction stacks. Or create a sign that can stand up at the end of a row of books. Where better to grab readers who might want to hear more about books than in the fiction stacks? This is particularly true for the new releases.

When possible, give patrons the information in a format they can take with them. Flyers are good, but bookmarks are even better. Don't let them just lie on the circulation counter, however. They'll ultimately become part of the furniture. Convince the circulation staff to stuff them in books and say, "Here's some information about our new booktalking program." If the staff is enthusiastic, it will carry over to the patrons. Remember to be redundant. Patrons, like us, need to read and hear about something a number of times before it sinks in.

Spread It Around

Once you've got your place posted, it's time to take your message on the road. Here's where posters come in handy. I've found that the smaller the poster, the easier it is for a business to display it. Also, some towns have sign ordinances that limit the amount of signage they are able to display in the window so go for an 8.5 x 11" or 11 x 17" size. You probably do this for every program the library has, so you know what to do. Sweep the streets and ask businesses to display your poster. Be a little more attentive to those businesses that serve the population you're after. If there's a bookstore in town, make an appointment with the manager for five minutes of her time. Big chain bookstores usually have a community relations coordinator that you can talk to. Take a poster and a stack of bookmarks or your business cards and explain briefly what you're about. Offer to do a program on the premises. Emphasize any particular audiences, such as book clubs, that you think would be particularly interested. Please don't walk in uninvited and attempt a spiel. We're all busy people, and interruptions are not warmly welcomed. Call in advance.

While you're cruising town, don't neglect office buildings. There are people in them, congregating in lunchrooms and at the water cooler. Drop off a poster with a brief memo attached to the human resources department and ask that it be posted in the staff lounge.

Take It to Cyberspace

If your library or agency has a Web site, and most do these days, there's another opportunity for you to spread the word. The same information you are using for your posters and bookmarks will work, but add a visual element if you can. Scan a photo of you actually talking to a rapt group and use that. Or use a standard black-and-white head shot. Anything you can do to personalize the message will make it more appealing.

I was startled when soon after I started my current job, the community relations coordinator encouraged me to book a session at a local photography studio so that the library would have a photo for publicity purposes. I asked the photographer for a more casual, approachable shot rather than a somber corporate pose. I have been surprised at how often that photo has been called into play. Not only does it go out on library publicity, but groups that I speak to sometimes ask for a photo to put in their newsletter before the event.

Talk to your webmaster about where your booktalking information can be featured. Maybe it's programming, maybe it's resources for book groups, maybe it's in booklists and reading recommendations, maybe it's all of the above. Discuss the possibilities.

Find Discrete Audiences

There are lots of audiences out in your community just waiting for you. They just don't know it yet. To find them, check the community calendar section of the local newspaper. If your library has a meeting room that's used by the public, take a look at who is using it. You might have an audience in your own backyard. Senior centers, retirement communities, service and community organizations, book groups—the list goes on and on. See what's happening in your community and figure out where your potential audience is. I'll cover some ways to get your word out to specific groups in Chapter 9, "Booktalking to Adults," and Chapter 11, "Booktalking in Schools."

So there's a start. It's time to grab your bell and your parchment and go out and be the town crier for a while. Don't be shy—be excited. This is a gift you are giving to your community.

4

Taking the Call

Okay, so far, so good. You've identified your motivation, your message, and your audience. You've publicized your availability in all sorts of inventive ways, and you're waiting for the phone to ring. Now prepare yourself to give and gather all the necessary information when that call comes. There's nothing worse than being lost in the middle of an endless housing subdivision and being unable to find your booktalking venue because, in your excitement or the rush to get out the door, you forgot to get the phone number of the contact. It sounds too basic for words, but it happens. Trust me on this . . .

Prepare an introductory paragraph that describes what it is that you do. Your caller (or e-mail correspondent) may have some idea but may just know that you give a program about books. The word *booktalk* doesn't mean anything to most people. Script out how you will explain your program and what you do. This is the time to bring up restrictions, fees, and the like. If you offer different themes, then say so now. I say something like, "I generally talk for about forty-five minutes. I bring a mixed bag of books, both fiction and nonfiction, and focus on books that are not best-sellers. I like hidden treasures, books you might not have heard of. There is no fee, this is a service of the library system."

Also prepare a paragraph or two about yourself that you can e-mail or send. People may be glad to have a program, but they still want to know your credentials and who you are. Ack! Now *The Music Man* is running through my head, "I'm sorry, professor, but we need your credentials." But I digress . . .

If the caller wants to book you, hurrah! You've got a gig. Here are the questions to ask now:

- Name and phone number of contact
- Name and phone number of host or venue, if different

- Location of venue and driving directions
- Number of people expected
- Predominant age and gender of audience
- Amount of time allotted for the program
- When the program begins
- When you are expected to arrive
- Whether a bio or a photo of you is needed for a newsletter or publicity, and if so, where it should be sent

Repeat back all that information and summarize, again, what you will do. Develop and use an automatic confirmation process. I call several days before the booktalk and reconfirm. Say that in your original conversation and put it on your calendar to do on the appropriate day.

I mentioned before how handy it is to have a professional black-and-white photo of yourself available that you can scan and e-mail or send out. Let me encourage you again to have this done. It adds a measure of professionalism to your program, and I think you'll be surprised how often there will be a call for it. Now don't get all queasy on me and start thinking about how much you hate getting your picture taken. Hardly anyone over the age of twelve is crazy about being photographed. But it's a great way to begin a connection with your audience. Why do you think realtors have their faces on just about everything from their "for sale" signs to their business cards? It gives the customer another way of connecting with them. Now you have more than just a name to work with. You can't help but look at those photos and begin thinking, "She looks nice. I could work with her to find a house to buy." Or "He looks so serious and trustworthy. I'd like him to list my house." It's business and it works. Nobody's looking for a glamour shot, just a photo to show your potential audience you're somebody with whom they can connect.

Many organizations will invite you to a meal in conjunction with their meetings. This is totally up to you, your time constraints, and your dietary preferences. There are advantages and disadvantages both ways. I don't have a set response to this; it just depends on what my day looks like. I sometimes skip a breakfast offer, just because it's difficult for me to get there that much earlier. I often accept a luncheon invitation. The logistics are easier, and it's often instructive to observe the dynamics going on in the group during the meal and the meeting. Sometimes I can pick up information to customize my booktalks just by watching. Plus, if you tend to be nervous, it can put you at ease to be with the group for a little bit before you're on. Dinner invitations really vary. Rush hour traffic is a bear in my neck of the woods, so that figures into it. I'm not crazy about eating a heavy meal before I speak, so that can be an issue as well.

Whatever you decide, get the correct information for when you should be there. Find out when the meal starts, when the meeting starts, and when your program begins. Tell the organizer when to expect you so there's no confusion. I learned this the hard way. On one occasion I walked into a room to give a booktalk right on time only to find that the organizer had expected me earlier and was now pale and sweaty, thinking I wasn't going to arrive. I knew I was going to be there on time, but he didn't. I've spent enough time waiting on tenterhooks for people I've booked to do a library program to show up that I should have known better. It's a terrible thing to look at your gathered audience, wondering where your presenter is. You start mentally reviewing your entertainment skills. Can I juggle? Tap dance? Sing arias? Just what am I going to do with this audience if my program doesn't show up? You get the picture. A little extra communication goes a long way toward relieving stress for all concerned. Now I say in my original conversation and in the confirmation, "I'm sorry I can't make it for lunch, but I'll be glad to do a thirty-minute program. I'll be there at 12:20 p.m. and ready to start at 12:30 p.m."

On the following page, you'll find a checklist I developed that covers the basic required information for an adult booktalk. I've been booktalking for a hundred years, and I still use this form. Make it easy on yourself; use a form or checklist and save your gray cells for the booktalk.

Booktalk Request

Name of group_____

Nature of group_____

Date and time of meeting _____

Location of meeting_____

Contact/phone_____

Estimated attendance_____

Gender or age predominance?_____

Desired length of talk: __ 30 minutes __45 minutes __ 60 minutes _____ other

Purpose of talk: __ general reading __ book group suggestions

Is biography or photo needed? ___ yes ____ no

 If so send to:

_____

_____

_____

_____

By this date:

Will map/directions be sent?

Reconfirm on (date):

Now that you've elicited the needs of the group, it's time to make your own needs known. If it's a large group or a large room, ask about the availability of a sound system. If you need a table to display your books, now is the time to say so. Do you expect your host to provide water for you? It's best to let him or her know.

If it's a school calling, there are a few other considerations as well. If you are not a school staff member, you should never booktalk in a class alone (see Chapter 11 "Rules for Schools"). Make sure this is understood. You'll want to clarify the ages of the group or groups you'll be talking to, as Sharon found out in this experience:

The worst booktalking experience I had had nothing to do with the kids but everything to do with the school librarian. She put a sixth grade class with a kindergarten class. This is an impossible split. I now make it clear that my booktalks are age appropriate and that they can mix up K–2 together and they can mix up 3–4 and 4–6, but never again will I allow such a horrendous combo."

I have been caught by surprise more than once by something it didn't occur to me to mention because it seemed obvious to me. Learn from Sharon's and my experiences that there is no such thing as obvious. Think about what you have to offer and what your needs are, then state them very clearly. Nicely, but clearly. On the following page, you'll find a booktalk request form adapted for school use.

School Booktalk Request

Name of school_____

Address_____

School district_____

Grade(s) _____

Date_____

Time/class period_____

Contact/phone_____

Estimated attendance_____

Length of class period_____

Desired length of talk_____

Purpose of talk: ___ general reading __ class assignment on_____

_____

Other_____

Will map/directions be sent?

Reconfirm the week before on (date):

Remember That You're Human

While your phone is ringing off the hook and you're happily taking bookings, don't forget that you're not a robot. There is a limit to how many booktalks you can successfully do in a day without collapsing. You'll need to experiment to see what works best for you. I know many public librarians who can go into a school and do booktalks for class after class throughout the school day. I discovered early on that I'm not one of them. Three booktalks in a row is what works for me. After that I can't remember what I've said to whom about what book, or even if I've done that book for that class. I no longer have to energy to flex and vamp if I need to—and you almost always need to. I'll happily revisit a school several times if that's what it takes, but I'll only do three booktalks a day. I can hear you sneering and hollering out there about logistics and time constraints and windows of opportunity. I realize that life isn't always perfect, but I just don't think the world needs any more booktalk martyrs. You want to give every class your best, and that can't happen when you're at the end of your string.

Also don't forget you need breaks. Mary learned this the hard way:

 My worst booktalking experience was really a matter of not paying close attention to the scheduling. When I set up the schedule for myself and my assistant at a large middle school in Cleveland, it wasn't until we arrived at the school and were reviewing the schedule that I realized we were both scheduled in classes all day with not even a lunch break. I made last-minute arrangements for both of us to cut two classes short in order to get lunch. Even so, at the end of the day we were both exhausted. After that we arranged to be at the school two days, and each of us took a half day each day. I also always wrote out the schedules with times and ensured we had a good lunch break."

It's the job of your contact to utilize your skills, but don't expect them to be your mom. It's your job to look after your own needs and make sure you have what it takes to give your best to your audience.

The Golden Rules of Booktalking

Most booktalkers agree that there are certain golden rules of booktalking. No matter how individual your style or how esoteric your choice of titles, these core elements remain constant. So here they are—the Golden Rules of Booktalking Success:

Golden Rule Number One:

Read the Book

Read the book. Sounds basic doesn't it? It is. But it doesn't get more critical. If you are not willing to read (and reread) every book that you booktalk, then put down this book and go have coffee. Nothing else I have to say matters. The whole point of booktalking is to share the enthusiasm you feel for a book with others. You can't have enthusiasm for a book you haven't read.

Let me be even more clear about this. Reading the jacket blurb is not reading the book. I've heard a "booktalk" where the speaker read the blurb word for word. It was excruciating. Did I run right out to read the book? You can easily answer that question correctly and win Double Jeopardy! Not only did I not read the book, I was sorry that this well-intentioned presenter had wasted both her time and mine.

Reading the reviews, no matter how lengthy and comprehensive, is not reading the book. Hearing about the book from a friend, colleague, or patron is not reading the book. Knowing that a book is popular because dozens of patrons have checked it out is not reading the book.

You must read the book to construct and deliver a booktalk properly. You must read the book to have any credibility with your audience. Woe betide you on the day that an eager teenager shouts out, "Did you *really* read all those books?" (and I promise you this will happen) and you can't honestly and confidently answer yes. It's a sad thing to see such a golden opportunity blown to smithereens. And it's not only teens who may challenge you. If there's anyone of any age in your audience who has read one of the books you are talking about, depend on the fact that they will want to chat with you about it afterward. It's all very well to portray the quirky sensuality of Lily Prior's *La Cucina* but how *did* you like the part when l'Inglese ate the oysters off Rosa's tummy? Read the book.

Can you pass on information about a book that you haven't read? Sure, that's an important part of readers' advisory. But we're not talking about readers' advisory at this moment, we're talking booktalking, and to do a booktalk, you must read the book.

Golden Rule Number Two

Like the Books You Booktalk

Like the books. Why in the world would you talk about books you don't like anyway? It makes no sense. Booktalking is a personal process—a person-to-person process. You establish camaraderie with your audience and share books you truly love. They'll try them, or not, based on not only what you have to say about the book, but how they feel about you. Being personal is the point. If your audience didn't want your personal recommendations, they could stay home and read the *New York Times Book Review.*

There is only one exception to this rule that I can think of. Sometimes youth services librarians are called upon to booktalk all the titles nominated for a given award, and sometimes there's a clinker in there. I'll talk about how to handle this situation in Chapter 10, "Booktalking to Children and Teens." In the mean time, talk about books you love and let your passion for them shine through.

Golden Rule Number Three

Know Your Audience

Know your audience. We'll talk about this concept lots more later on. As you might guess, booktalking to folks in a retirement home is much different from booktalking to junior high school students, just as booktalking to middle school students is different from booktalking to third graders. The basic skills are the same, but the techniques vary. Always know to whom you are talking. (Why does Lily Tomlin pop into my head just now? "Is this the party to whom I am speaking?") This will affect your choice of books, the structure of your booktalk, and your approach. Know about your audience in the general terms of the needs of its particular age or developmental group. Know your audience in the specifics of age, gender, interests, and background. As much as you possibly can, know your audience.

Golden Rule Number Four

Booktalk

Booktalk. Booktalk? What, is there an echo in here? Aren't we talking about booktalking? Absolutely. That's why I want you to be careful to booktalk. I don't want you to review the books or reprise the book or rehash the book. Have you ever sat through a coffee break recitation of last night's television episode—scene by scene by scene? Endless, wasn't it? Booktalking is not telling the whole plot of the book, neither is it tendering a review of the book. Oral book reviewing was hot stuff in the 1940s and 1950s, and if you choose to do it, go for it. But don't mistake it for booktalking.

Booktalks are certainly subjective, but they aren't evaluative. Don't tell your audience it's a great book. If you didn't think it was terrific, why are you booktalking it? Booktalking is giving just enough information to convey the feeling of the book. You want your audience to be intrigued by the book and interested enough to investigate further, which brings us to the next golden rule of booktalking.

Golden Rule Number Five

Don't Tell the Ending!

I know this has happened to you at some time. You overheard a conversation that totally destroyed the suspense of that boffo new blockbuster movie you were going to see. Or even worse, a friend (now a former friend) was so excited about the ending of that new mystery that she told you *all* about it, even though the book was sitting on your bedside table, waiting tantalizingly for you to have the time for a treat. You get the picture. Don't put your audience in the position of having to stick their fingers in their ears and hum. Don't tell the ending!

Don't make me explain this any further. Just know that severe karmic penalties are involved if you break this rule. Don't tell the ending!

Golden Rule Number Six

Leave a List

Leave a list of the books you talked about for your audience. Be kind to your audience and the librarians and booksellers who will be dealing with them in the next few days. Don't force them to scribble notes on the backs of their hands. Don't put them in a position of having to say, "All I know is it's a mystery and the word *snow* is in the title . . . but it sounded like a terrific book!" Give them a list. Put the titles and the authors and a brief sentence identifying the book. Don't worry about intricate bibliographical information. Also include your name, library or agency, and contact information. You'll want them to be able to write you a fulsome thank you note (which you can then show to your boss) and contact you again to repeat your stellar performance another time. Who knows how many other groups are represented in the audience of the crowd you just spoke to?

So there they are. The six golden rules of booktalking. The six supports upon which you craft your booktalk. Everything else having to do with your booktalks you can shape to your druthers, comfort level, and personality. All you have to do is promise me now that you'll always, always booktalk, and not review books that you've read and loved; that you'll know as much about your audience as is humanly possibly; and that you'll leave your dear audience a list of the books you've talked about. All the while you will never, ever reveal the ending of a book.

Here's a note I received after booktalking to a women's group. I particularly like it because she let me know that I was following my own "Golden Rules":

 Dear Chapple,
The women would like to express their thanks for a delightful program. You gave just enough highlights of each book that made it interesting, also wanting to read the favorites they had marked on their brochure. We're looking forward to another program with you . . ."

6

Choosing Your Books

The Booktalker's Bible

Okay, here comes the fun part, actually deciding what titles you want to booktalk to a given group. Some folks have a standard list of titles that they booktalk, period. This goes for any audience. They do new books or literary fiction, and that's their standard presentation. I am not a huge fan of that approach. I want my audience to be receptive to me and as engaged as possible, so I tailor each booktalk around what I know about the audience. My booktalks may have similar components, but they are rarely exactly the same. I may have an active repertoire of 120 books that I booktalk. From that list I'll pull twelve to fifteen for each group, and it will vary each time. I choose books based on what I know about the audience, how much time I have to speak, and what I can tie in to current news events or trends in publishing. The time of year will impact what books I choose. If spring training has just started or the Mariners are making a run for the playoffs, I'll likely include a baseball book like *The Oldest Rookie* by Jim Morris or Terry Kay's *Taking Lottie Home*. If it's the dead of winter, I may choose to talk about *Winterdance* by Gary Paulsen or Steve Hamilton's mystery set in Michigan's Upper Peninsula, *A Cold Day in Paradise*. If tensions are high in the Middle East, I might include *Zoya's Story* by Zoya with John Follain and Rita Cristofari or *Nine Parts of Desire* by Geraldine Brooks.

When I'm booktalking to adults I tend not to talk about best-sellers or books that are all the current buzz. I figure my audience can read the best-seller list in the newspaper as well as I can. I'm not doing them any particular service by telling them about those books. And, alas, Barbara Kingsolver probably isn't sitting at home breathlessly waiting for the exposure I can give her. Besides, unless your library has a lot more money that ours does, there will probably be dozens, or even hundreds, of people in the holds queue for a best-selling title. You will have generated a lot of enthusiasm for a book that your audience will have to wait for patiently while other patrons get their turn. That's no fun for anybody. I try to emphasize lesser-known works and emerging authors, but mostly I talk about books that I've enjoyed and about which I can be genuinely enthusiastic.

I encourage you to read broadly and to include as many genres as you can into your booktalks. Literary fiction is all fine and well, but nobody wants to eat broccoli all the time. There is no shame in booktalking popular fiction. A sassy romance by Jennifer Crusie might be just the ticket for capturing the interest of a group of young professional women. A hard-driven, page-turning thriller like *Vertical Run* by Joseph R. Garber might speak to the fellows in a big way. And who can resist a great mystery, be it the tense *Darkness Peering* by Alice Blanchard or something with a lighter touch like Michael Bond's *Monsieur Pamplemousse*? The more diverse your repertoire, the more credence you have with your audience. If that crusty old gentleman who reads nothing but westerns hears you wax rhapsodic over the estimable Elmer Kelton, he might be inclined to think you know a thing or two about books. And, of course, you do.

I'll admit that I place some titles on each and every list—at least for a while—either because I think a book has wide appeal or because I'm so deeply in love with it that I think everybody needs to know about it. So let's talk a little bit about that magic word—appeal.

Identifying Appeal

You know the standard genres: horror, science fiction, westerns, horror, romance, mystery, fantasy, and so on. But within genres there are appeal factors to consider. In readers' advisory circles, appeal is a big deal. Go to just about any standard work on readers' advisory, and you'll find some learned theories on what it is about given types of books that make people want to read them. Readers' advisory gurus Nancy Pearl, Joyce Saricks, and Duncan Smith all make a compelling case for there being basic components of a book that draw readers. What I've drawn from their work are these five basic factors: plot or action, characters, language or writing style, setting, and the impact of the book on the reader—what Duncan Smith calls affect.

Before you start booktalking, it's helpful to give this some thought. Consider books you've read and particularly enjoyed. What particularly captured you? Was it the well-developed or quirky characters? I always think of books like Adriana Trigiani's *Big Stone Gap* or John Welter's *I Want to Buy a Vowel* that feature a town full of eccentrics, crackpots, and nutcases. Or there's *Fleur de Leigh's Life of Crime* by Diane Leslie in which each chapter revolves around a different one of Fleur's peculiar nannies.

Perhaps it was the fast moving or intricately woven plot. Author Don McQuinn cracked me up when he compared reading Robert Ludlum to falling down a flight of stairs. You just can't stop in the middle—and if you do, you're toast. For my money, plotmaster Jeffrey Deaver is one of the masters of this category, and I love to booktalk *The Devil's Teardrop*.

Are books that you love set so vividly in a particular place and time that it felt like the setting was another character? Don't you agree that Victorian London plays a critical role in Anne Perry's Thomas Monk or Inspector Pitt novels? And what about the role of nineteenth-century New Orleans in Barbara Hambly's excellent Benjamin January series? When I read the first in the series, *A Free Man of Color*, I was totally transported by the sights, sounds, and smells of New Orleans in 1833.

Maybe it was the beautiful language that stirred your soul. I remember Nancy Pearl saying how delighted she is to read a book with language so exquisite that it causes her to pause and admire it. I was a little dubious about this being a likely scenario for me until I came across Leif Enger's *Peace Like a River*. Reading this charming novel, I did indeed find myself stopping frequently to savor a particularly splendid turn of phrase.

I think it's extremely useful to know your own reading patterns when it comes to appeal factors. It was an epiphany for me to realize that what spoke to me most in a book was the plot and characters. Suddenly I realized why elegant, moody literary fiction that featured gorgeous writing and not much plot so often failed to engage me. And it explained why I could forgive almost anything of an author whose characters made me laugh. I felt vindicated somehow, or at least liberated, to know why there were acclaimed books that I just couldn't make myself read. The appeal factors were all wrong for me.

No matter how eclectic a reader you are (and I hope you are), there are certain elements in books that particularly speak to you in a soul-satisfying way. Michele freely admits that she reads romances because she wants a happy ending, and that's just part of the definition of that genre. And if an old house gets fixed up or a frazzled life gets put in order at the same time, then that's heaven for Michele. I know just what she means. Sometimes nothing beats the new lady of the manor whipping the old place into shape. You know those scenes—walls gleaming with new paint, furniture shining with beeswax, and fresh flowers everywhere . . . and only the servants are tired.

35

I figure food must be an appeal factor for a huge number of people. Look at all the fiction that's out now that has recipes included. Personally, there's nothing I love more than having a great meal and fine wine along with a character. But I digress.

My point is to think about the appeal of books you read in general and the books you're thinking of booktalking in particular. I think it's important to bring a mixed bag, literally, with lots of different genres and appeal factors represented.

Don't Forget Nonfiction

As broad and varied as the appeal of fiction is, it's not the only booktalk fodder in your literary pantry. Nonfiction and memoirs are terrific choices for booktalks and will often capture readers who would not touch a work of fiction, literary or otherwise. A good example is Jon Krakauer's recounting of the tragic Everest expedition, *Into Thin Air.* I also like to use Erik Larson's *Isaac's Storm,* a compelling story about the devastating hurricane in Galveston in 1900. And then there's Caroline Alexander's *Endurance* about the Shackelton expedition in the Antarctic, an exciting read made spectacular by Frank Hurley's original photos from the expedition.

I have a particular soft spot for memoirs and biographies. There's just something about the fact that person you're reading about had no idea at the time how his or her life would turn out; that it would all be okay (or not) makes for compelling reading, and I enjoy using them in booktalks. So to get you started down the memoir trail, here's a list of my favorite booktalkable biographies.

Mesmerizing Memoirs

📖 *Ava's Man* by Rick Bragg
> In this sequel to *All Over but the Shoutin',* Rick tells the story of his mother's father, Charlie Bundrum.

📖 *Bound Feet & Western Dress* by Pang-Mei Natasha Chang
> Intrigued by finding her family name in a Chinese history course, Natasha uncovers the astounding story of her great aunt.

📖 *The Cat Who Went to Paris* by Peter Gethers
> Peter Gethers didn't want a cat, but when he received a Scottish fold kitten as a gift, it was love at first purr.

📖 *The Ditchdigger's Daughters: A Black Family's Astonishing Success Story* by Yvonne S. Thornton, MD

> Donald Thornton, a ditchdigger in Monmouth, New Jersey, decided all five of his daughters would become doctors.

📖 *Ethel and Ernest: A True Story* by Raymond Briggs

> The story of Briggs's parents' courtship and marriage—in graphic novel format.

📖 *A Girl Named Zippy* by Haven Kimmel

> A memoir of "growing up small" in Mooreland, Indiana, in the 1960s and 1970s.

📖 *I Will Be Cleopatra* by Zoe Caldwell

> Acclaimed actress Caldwell recounts events in her life from her Australian childhood to her portrayal of Cleopatra in 1967.

📖 *Limbo* by A. Manette Ansay

> From childhood, Ansay trained to become a concert pianist. But at nineteen, a mysterious muscle disorder forced her to give up the piano; by twenty-one she couldn't grip a pen or walk across a room.

📖 *Lost in Place* by Mark Salzman

> Inspired by Kung Fu movies, Mark decides at thirteen to become a wandering Zen monk. This proves challenging in suburban Connecticut. (This is a great one to use with teens.)

📖 *Memories of a Lost Egypt* by Colette Rossant

> Colette spends her growing up years with her Egyptian grandparents in a Belle Epoch mansion on the Nile in pre–World War II Cairo.

📖 *Space: A Memoir* by Jesse Lee Kercheval

> Jesse Lee's family moves to Florida just as the preparation for the moonshot is in full swing.

📖 *Stuffed: Adventures of a Restaurant Family* by Patricia Volk

> An unsparing and hilarious account of family and food.

📖 *Tender at the Bone* by Ruth Reichl

> A restaurant critic and food editor's delicious memoirs.

📖 *Train Go, Sorry* by Leah Hager Cohen
> One year in the life of New York City's Lexington School for the Deaf.

📖 *Uphill Walker* by Madeleine Blais
> In 1952, Madeleine's father dies suddenly, leaving behind a pregnant wife and five young children.

Depending on the group, I'll weight a presentation with a certain type of book. If you're speaking to a book group, you're going to want to include more literary titles with themes and characters that lend themselves to discussion. This is probably going to be a much different selection of books than you would take to a Rotary meeting, for instance. When I know that a group is made up primarily of men, I'll include more thrillers, sports, and true adventure. I'll talk about different audiences in a little more depth in Chapter 9, "Booktalking to Adults."

Another point you need to bear in mind is both cautionary and celebratory. Duncan Smith points out that even when we read the same book, we each read a different book. People bring their own life experiences to the story and will pull different things from it. To my mind, that's another great thing about booktalking, you get to share not only the story that the author has written, but, in some basic way, your own story as well.

So Many Books, So Little Time

How many books should you bring to booktalk? How long will it take you? It varies, of course, from person to person, but I find that 12 to 15 books give me enough material for a forty-five-minute booktalking presentation. Eighteen titles takes me through an hour. You'll want to think about and plan for the unexpected, however. Chance, a children's librarian, puts it this way:

> The thing I always tried to do when asked to booktalk was to over-prepare. If I was asked to talk for a half an hour, which to me seems about as bearable length of time as you can reasonably expect your average elementary school student to listen to booktalks, I always brought enough material to talk for an hour. Why? What if the first five sure-fire winners are five short-circuiting clunkers? Having more than enough to talk about will ensure you the flexibility you need when certain books aren't working. What if the half hour of material is used up in fifteen minutes? It has happened that books I thought

would take longer to get through, even after rehearsing, go much faster with a live group. Now, this may mean that I was talking *way* too fast, or it may mean that the insightful questions that my dynamic talk was designed to elicit did not come up. Either way, I am ready with more to talk about. Now, don't get me wrong, I'm not just trying to fill up time, I am trying to make sure that I have *all* the props, bits, shticks, and tricks with me as I work through a talk. One thing that always happens is that serendipity strikes during every talk. Connections between authors and themes that were not apparent during the preparation time become dazzling examples of great literature and graceful segues from one book to the next. So, the short answer is, the more you prepare, the more you know, and therefore, the better prepared and less nervous you will be."

Preparing Your List

The list I've told you to bring need not be complicated. Basically, you just want to give enough information so that the book can be found. Author and title is generally plenty. If you are booktalking to colleagues, you may want to add more detailed bibliographic information. One librarian I know adds the birth and death dates of the author and the publication date when she's booktalking classics. Usually, author and title is enough.

Now add a little something to trigger a memory of what the book is about. This is not a full-fledged readers' annotation, it's just a sentence or a phrase identifying the book. In this instance, the less said, the better. You don't want your audience members reading your lovely annotations when they should be listening to your glorious booktalks.

I order my lists by title. You may choose to order your lists according to author or in the order you plan to talk about them. Which brings us to . . .

Making Your Program Flow

When you're putting together the list of titles you want to booktalk, think about the balance of the program and the order in which you want to present your books. If you're a fan of clever segues to tie one book to another, then by all means incorporate them into your talk. I don't think it's hugely important that one book tie into the next. Keep a balance of lighter titles and more serious books, brief booktalks and those that are more involved. It's not a great idea to do three or four terribly profound or sad books in a row and have your audience wondering if they've mistakenly wandered into a meeting of the Lugubrious Book Club. Nor do you want to make a jarring change from a tragic story to a highly comic one.

I like to start and end a program with booktalks that are tried and true, ones I'm sure I can deliver with panache. You want to grab your audience right away and let them get comfortable with you. A polished booktalk does that for you. When a good actor walks on stage, he gives his audience an immediate measure of comfort just by his presence and assurance. That's what you need to establish. An actor who communicates to the audience that he's not sure he can remember his lines makes for an uneasy audience and a fitful performance.

I save booktalks for titles that are intimate or sensitive for the later part of my talk. For instance, I love to booktalk Joni Rodger's memoir *Bald in the Land of Big Hair,* particularly to an adult female audience. I use a funny scene in which Joni's attempts to masturbate are thwarted by the alarm on her chemo drip, which brings the whole family running but I'll only do this booktalk later on in my presentation when I've built a bond with the audience and we're feeling comfortable with one another.

To Tote or Not to Tote

Now that you've chosen the books you want to talk about and the order in which you want to present them, think about transporting them. Some find that toting around fifteen to twenty books is more than they care to do. Of course, if you're checking books out on site, that's your only option. Some librarians just take the book jackets and leave the books at home or the library. Martha has an interesting solution. She makes a color photocopy of the jacket and laminates it. She takes it one step further and attaches her notes about the book to the back of the copy. She says they are easy to file, easy to grab, and easy to transport. Another librarian glues a color copy of the book jacket to a piece of book-sized foam core, which is like poster board laminated to a quarter inch of Styrofoam. This solution keeps the book jacket from falling over.

I've known people who scan the jackets and turn their booktalk into a PowerPoint presentation. This can be an interesting way to present books, but in my opinion, it's not booktalking. You've taken the focus away from you and on the projected computer screen; you've lost the ability to build a personal rapport.

This is again an area of personal style and comfort. I've tried some of these alternative methods, and they just don't work for me. I seem to need the book in my hand. It gives me comfort to know that I can open to any page and review a character's name or plot point. I like the weight of it and the fact that I can set it on a tabletop for display. I like the fact that audience members can eyeball the books while I'm talking and see if they are big or small, thick or thin, and what the cover looks like. In essence, the books share the spotlight. I also like it when audience members can come up afterward and thumb through the books, check out the illustrations, and sample a paragraph or two to see if it speaks to them.

Toting Your Notes

If I have the book with me, I don't take notes. If I need to check the book for a piece of information I can. There's no sin in taking a stack of note cards with you so that you have an emergency backup if your memory fails you. It's common practice for booktalkers to tape note cards or put Post-its on the back of the book they're talking about. Let me just say I hate this practice. It's neither subtle nor stealthy. It's plain to the audience that the notes are there, especially if you refer to them. I think it's distracting and sends a pretty strong message that although you say these are great books, they didn't really make much of an impression on you. Jeani, an experienced booktalker, agrees with me:

My one piece of advice for booktalking: don't tape your booktalks to the back of the book. It can be distracting and discourage you from more effectively memorizing a booktalk. Plus, at least once during the course of a day of booktalking, a student would ask me what I had on the back of my book. I tried different responses, but not one elicited interest or sympathy. It impresses students when they see you talking about a book from memory. They are also impressed when they find out that you have read every book you are booktalking."

Build a Booktalking Collection

If space and money permit, and you booktalk often, consider creating a booktalking collection for yourself. I used to pull my booktalk books exclusively from the library's collection, which limited me to books that were checked in at just the moment I needed them and eliminated any title that had even one person in the holds queue. Because I booktalk several times a month, this just didn't turn out to be an expedient method for me, so I started building my own booktalking collection. Now when I read a book that I'd like to add to my booktalking repertoire, I check on its paperback status on Amazon.com, *Books in Print*, or *Forthcoming Books*. If I can find a date the paperback is due out, I put a note in my tickler file for that month to purchase the book. If I can't find a date, I just put a note in my file for six months out. I occasionally buy a hardback (if I just can't wait!), but I usually stick to trade paperbacks, which makes my budget for this reasonable and my book bag a little lighter.

In my former life as a young adult librarian, I was in a position in which three of us were doing young adult services, including booktalking for an entire county—thirty-seven branches. Whenever any one of us would find a book we loved to booktalk, we'd buy five or six copies of the mass-market paperback and add it to our joint collection. When any of us went out to booktalk, we'd pull multiple copies of titles from this collection and deposit them in the closest branch library to our booktalking site. When these titles stopped moving, the branch staff returned them, and back they'd go into the booktalk collection. It was a great system.

Additional Reading

On Readers' Advisory

📕 Saricks, Joyce G., and Nancy Brown. *Readers' Advisory Service in the Public Library*, second edition. Chicago: American Library Association, 1997.

📕 Saricks, Joyce G. *The Readers' Advisory Guide to Genre Fiction.* Chicago: American Library Association, 2001.
> Fifteen major genres are covered here with their characteristics, key authors, and "sure bets" that consistently appeal to a wide variety of readers.

📕 Shearer, Kenneth D. *The Readers' Advisor's Companion.* Englewood, Colo.: Libraries Unlimited, 2001.

Essays on readers' advisory from the philosophical to the pragmatic.

On Exploring Genres and Reading Suggestions

📖 Craughwell, Thomas. *Great Books for Every Book Lover: 2002 Great Reading Suggestions for the Discriminating Bibliophile*. New York: Black Dog & Leventhal, 1998.

This is a great book to browse when you're looking for booktalk candidates. It's divided into categories that range from "Women of Substance" to "Great Gossip."

📖 Herald, Diana Tixier. *Genreflecting: A Guide to Reading Interests in Genre Fiction*, fifth edition. Englewood, Colo.: Libraries Unlimited, 2000.

This is a great one to help you find good reads in every genre.

📖 Pearl, Nancy (with assistance from Martha Knappe and Chris Higashi). *Now Read This: A Guide to Mainstream Fiction, 1978–1998*. Englewood, Colo.: Libraries Unlimited, 1999.

A listing of literary fiction and their readalikes grouped by appeal factors. There is also information on appeal factors and how to conduct a readers' advisory interview.

📖 Pearl, Nancy. *Now Read This II*. Greenwood Village, Colo.: Libraries Unlimited/Greenwood Publishing Group, 2002.

More contemporary titles grouped according to appeal factors. A companion to Pearl's previous volume.

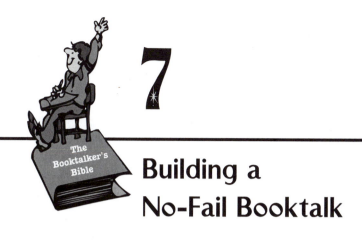

7

Building a
No-Fail Booktalk

Okay, it's time. Enough of this talk about books. Let's start booktalking.

What to Look for While You're Reading

Building the perfect booktalk starts while you're reading the book. Create an awareness that sits in the back of your mind and watches for great booktalk material. Watch for scenes that are particularly interesting or characters with great lines. Look for passages that exemplify the mood of the book. Pay attention to what makes you laugh and what makes you cry. When it's a book that compels you to tell your colleagues or friends about it, what parts do you mention?

When you've finished a book, take a few minutes while it's fresh in your mind and think about the appeal factors of the book. Was it the crazy characters? Was it the suspenseful plot? Maybe it was the setting, or maybe it was the humor or tone of the book that appealed to you.

When I complete a book I enter it in my reading log, which for me is just a blank book. For you it might be note cards or a computer journal. Instead of crafting an annotation at this point, I write a stream of consciousness about the book. I note the basics of the plot and my favorite characters or scenes. I make comments about the writing style. If it reminds me of other books, I'll write that down as well. I'll note the genre and think about the general appeal factors of the book: plot, setting, characters, language, affect. If there are passages in the book that I particularly like, I'll copy them. I'll also write down any quotes from the characters that I found entertaining or revealing (with the page numbers so I can refer back to them). All this really doesn't take much time, and it will give you a solid background for your booktalk. You can look back on your reactions to a book and begin to formulate your booktalk. Often, the booktalk starts forming in my mind while I'm writing my notes on a book. If it does, I just keep writing and jot the booktalk down in my log to be polished later. The more you can record while the book is fresh, the better off you are.

Finding the Hook

Somewhere in all the parts of the book that appealed to you will be a scene, circumstance, or plot device that will illustrate what you most like about the book and that will beg to be communicated to others. It will give the flavor of the book and provide an impetus to read the book, but it will not give away the ending (remember the Golden Rule!). This is the hook, and it is the foundation on which the rest of the booktalk rests. I know a librarian who maintains that the best hooks for any presentation—booktalk or otherwise—have to do with fire, water, sex, greed, and fear. Well, that's certainly one approach, and she might not be too far off base.

While you're reading, or right after you've finished the book, search out your hook. Once you've found it, the rest of the booktalk falls into place. You build to the hook by giving just enough background for it to make sense.

Here's a sample of one of my booktalks that has a straightforward, plot-related hook:

📖 *A Darker Place* by Laurie King

Anne Waverly is a respected university professor. Her academic specialty is alternative religious movements. Few people know that Anne's interest is rooted in her own involvement with a religious community as a young woman, an involvement that had a tragic end. But the FBI knows, and they occasionally ask her to infiltrate suspicious cults to determine their stability. Four times Anne has done this for the FBI, and each effort has left emotional and physical scars. She is loath to accept another assignment, reluctant to drag her achy forty-eight-year-old body into the fray again, doubtful of her ability to transform herself into the persona of a middle-aged seeker of Truth and Light. But seduced by the photos of the children in The Change compound, she reluctantly agrees, vowing that this assignment will be her last—and it very nearly is. That's *A Darker Place* by Laurie King.

This brief booktalk is less than a minute long, but it gives an inkling of who this Anne Waverly is, offers a glimpse of an intriguing situation, and leaves you wondering what will happen. That's the hook. To find out what happens to Anne, in whom you now have an interest, you must read the book.

Some books have plots that were made in booktalk hook heaven, and these will probably form the crux of your booktalking presentation, just because they are indeed no-fail. Here is another example:

📖 *Under the Beetle's Cellar* by Mary Willis Walker

> The last thing Walter Deming expected early in the morning on a country road near Jezreel, Texas, was a bunch of men with AK-47s surrounding the school bus he was driving. He and eleven children were taken to the Hearth Jezreelite compound and buried inside yet another bus. They have now been underground for forty-six days. Walter does his best to calm and placate the children, but he doesn't see himself as a kid kind of guy. He's a Vietnam vet, a loner, who drives a school bus to supplement his income as a gardener. The only thing Walter wanted out of life was no more trouble. Every morning he and the children endure a visit from Samuel Mordecai, the prophet of the Jezreelites. He calls the children "Lambs of God" and tells them they are being purified in readiness for the end of the world. He preaches wild, rambling sermons to them for hours on end.
>
> Molly Cates is a journalist who interviewed Mordecai for a magazine article two years earlier. He scared her to death. She really doesn't want any more to do with him, but like the rest of the world, she is riveted to the news coverage of the kidnapped children. Her editor convinces her that she is the perfect person to do another piece on Mordecai, that it's the opportunity of a lifetime, a Pulitzer Prize in the making. She finally, reluctantly, agrees. She digs into her research, and what she discovers convinces her that the children and Walter have only four days to live. That's *Under the Beetle's Cellar* by Mary Willis Walker.

Clearly plot-related hooks are the easiest to build. There's nothing quite so satisfying as that cliffhanging ending. But if you do that for every one of the books you booktalk in a single presentation, you may be cheerfully murdered by your audience, so make sure you vary your approaches and the hooks in your booktalking session.

Perhaps it's the premise that is the most intriguing part of the story. In that case, you'd be more likely to give an overview of the plot. Here's an example of a booktalk that has a broader scope:

📖 *Pope Joan* by Donna Woolfolk Cross

Johanna was born in Westphalia, in what is now Germany, in 814 AD. Her father was an English minister and her mother a Norsewoman he had met on one of his missionary trips. As she grew, Johanna, or Joan as she was called, showed a predilection that was unfortunate for a girl of that time. She loved to read. Now reading, for a girl, was not only frowned upon, it was considered ungodly, so it was a testament to Johanna's power of persuasion that she was able to entice her older brother to teach her how. A visiting cleric discovered Johanna's secret and was so impressed by her scholarship that he proposed she attend the Cathedral schola in a neighboring town. Joan's father, a severe man, was furious and humiliated at Joan's ability to read and would never have consented to her schooling except for one thing: the visiting cleric had arranged for Joan's younger brother John to attend school as well, something that he would never have achieved on his own, for John was no scholar. So Joan's father reluctantly agreed.

When Joan arrived at school, she thought she was in heaven. She could hardly believe that all of the books in the Cathedral library were available to her. She was treated badly by both her masters and her fellow students, all of whom were outraged at having a female in school, but Joan was willing to withstand the abuse as long as she could read and learn.

Not many years later, a series of circumstances led Joan, dressed in boys clothing, to knock at the door of a monastery and present herself as a monk. Joan lived there for thirteen years, becoming renowned as a scholar and healer. Eventually Joan made her way to Rome where, if you believe Donna Woolfolk Cross, she was elected Pope and served for two years.

Now this novel is a pretty intriguing story in and of itself, but what makes it even more interesting is Donna Cross's historical notes in the back of the book that tell you why she believes that Joan really did exist and actually did serve as Pope. It's her view that the Catholic Church has conveniently erased Joan from its history, not wanting to admit a woman was Pope. You can read *Pope Joan* for yourself and see what you think really happened. *Pope Joan* by Donna Woolfolk Cross.

Now if you were paying attention to the Golden Rules, you're wagging your finger at me, saying, "You told the ending! You told the ending!" Yes, I'm guilty as charged on this one. I did, however, tippytoe across some major plot twists in this booktalk because I didn't want to give away all the surprises. My main focus was Joan's background and the premise of her becoming Pope. The mystery of "did she or didn't she" is still there. This booktalk often elicits murmurs of interest from a female audience.

When a character is the thrust of your booktalk, you can build up the different facets of a character and then leave him or her at a crossroads. The plot is intriguing, but it's the character we want to know more about. Here's an example.

☐ *Miss Julia Speaks Her Mind* by Ann B. Ross

Miss Julia Springer, long-time church member and pillar of the community, has recently buried her likewise estimable husband, Wesley Lloyd Springer. Now Julia misses Wesley Lloyd right enough, but she's discovering that there are quite a few things she likes about being on her own. She can wear what she pleases, for one thing. Wesley Lloyd was always particular about what she wore. And she can eat what she pleases, without having to follow Wesley Lloyd's strict dictums about what dinner was to be. Best of all, she's learned to write a check. Now Wesley Lloyd, being a banker, was pretty careful with money, and he left Miss Julia a tidy sum. She's having a fine time spending some of it.

Miss Julia's life without Wesley Lloyd takes an unexpected turn one day when she opens the front door to find Hazel Marie Pickett and a youngster standing on her stoop. "I have to go get some trainin'," says Hazel Marie. "I know you're a good Christian woman and you'll do right by my boy." Then Hazel Marie runs off leaving a scrawny nine-year-old boy on Miss Julia's doorstep, a boy who is the spitting image of Wesley Lloyd. *Miss Julia Speaks Her Mind* by Ann B. Ross.

Building the Structure

A booktalk in its purest essence consists of these steps:

1. *The Beginning:* This is the entry into the book for your audience. It leads them to the book, gives them a chance to focus on this new book, this new topic. Often it's a sequel from the previous book. For *A Darker Place,* I talk briefly about Laurie King, the

Mary Russell books for which she is most noted, and the fact that *A Darker Place* is a stand-alone novel.

2. *The Lead-in:* This is the background you need to give the audience before you lead up to the hook. In *A Darker Place,* it's Anne's background and expertise and the circumstances that may lead her into danger. You need just enough for the hook to make sense. Notice that I painted Anne's background in broad strokes. I alluded to the tragedy in her past but didn't specify that her husband and child were killed.

3. *The Hook:* This is the critical scene that will entice them into the book to find out how it is resolved, to meet more of those wacky characters, or to enjoy more of the beautiful language. We know now that Anne has agreed to infiltrate The Change. Will she survive?

4. *The Close:* If your hook is strong enough, you may not need more and the closure will be unnecessary. I didn't use any closing comments for *A Darker Place* because the hook is so clear and so dramatic. Any additional comments would be anticlimactic. Sometimes, particularly if I'm talking to an adult audience, I may add a brief evaluative sentence or readalike comment. Following is an example. Notice how brief it is.

📕 *La Cucina: A Novel of Rapture* by Lily Prior

Rosa Fiore cooks when she's nervous—or upset or happy or just can't sleep. Rosa's cooking has been legendary in her small Sicilian town since she was a teenager. When Bartolemo, her first love, is killed, Rosa retreats first to the kitchen, cooking until the cupboards are bare, and then to Palermo where she becomes (gasp!) a librarian. Growing ever more corpulent and depressed, Rosa is shaken back to life when l'Inglese, an English chef and writer walks into her library. If you liked the quirky sensuality and magical realism of *Like Water for Chocolate,* you'll like *La Cucina* by Lily Prior.

You may have noticed by now that the title and author of the book are always the last things you say in a booktalk. This fixes it in minds of your audience, or just confirms it for those who didn't catch it at the beginning—or who didn't know they were interested until you got into the booktalk. It also serves as clear punctuation, "I'm done with this book now."

Here's another premise-based booktalk, with a little extra at the end:

📖 *Year of Wonders* by Geraldine Brooks

The young widow Anna Firth gladly took the journeyman tailor as a boarder. When he fell ill, she nursed him, but despite her best efforts, he died. His last words were to exhort Anna to burn all the clothes he had been making, instructions she passed on to the other villagers as each came to pick up their partially done garments. None did so, of course. Why waste good, new fabric? Soon the plague that killed the tailor was rife in the village. Inspired and persuaded by their charismatic vicar, the townsfolk agreed to quarantine themselves so as not to pass the contagion on to the neighboring villages. This is the story of the year it took for the plague to run its course. A year that Anna Firth called a Year of Wonders. This novel is based on the true story of the village of Eyam, Derbyshire, and it's one of my favorites of the year. *Year of Wonders* by Geraldine Brooks.

Notice that I did say that *Year of Wonders* was one of my favorites of the year. That's a personal connection, and it's perfectly okay to do. It's basically a comment on the book's impact on me. It's also fine to characterize a book as thrilling, suspenseful, funny, or any number of other adjectives that describe the impact of the book. What it's not okay to do is describe a book as good, wonderful, splendid, swell, great, or any other meaningless acclaim. You're not adding any information with these adjectives. Demonstrate with your booktalk why you like the book so much.

Writing Your Booktalk

So now you have an idea of what a booktalk looks, feels, and sounds like it's time to try your own. When you are first starting out, I recommend writing down your booktalk. My best booktalks happen when I write them. I don't always follow them verbatim, but writing them fixes the structure and the key points in my mind like nothing else. And it's easier to see what needs to be edited and cleaned up when your booktalk is in print in front of you. Also, if you have a written booktalk in your file, you can go back to a book after a long absence much more easily. For your first few booktalks, try the following process:

Write a rough draft. Craft a beginning, an introduction, lead up to your hook, deliver the hook, and close. When you are writing your booktalk, pay special attention to the beginning and the end. Elizabeth, a veteran children's librarian, writes out and memorizes the first sentence and the final sentence. She says those are the most important—and she's right. The first sentence captures your audience for you, and the last sentence sends them to the book. Just the right wording in those two key places can make your booktalk special. Even if you are writing in third person, concentrate on your characters experience or circumstance, or the setting if that's what you're focusing on. That's what makes it immediate. Do not under any circumstances start your booktalk with "This book is about . . ." That's neither immediate nor interesting. Make a positive, vivid, and intriguing statement about something.

- "Zippy was three years old before she spoke her first word." (*A Girl Named Zippy* by Haven Kimmel)
- "In 1936, Joey Margolis's Dad decamped with his secretary." (*The Last Days of Summer* by Steve Kluger)
- "To tell you the truth, Courtney had a bad attitude before the accident." (*Mind's Eye* by Paul Fleischman)
- "Have you ever wanted to take a flock of chickens and spin them around at 2.5 g just to see what would happen?" (*Great Mambo Chicken and the Transhuman Condition: Science Slightly Over the Edge* by Edward Regis.

Adding a Personal Touch

Sometimes I start or end a booktalk by referring to my own personal experience with a book or the author.

- "When I started *Miss Garnet's Angel* by Salley Vickers, I was positive I knew this story."
- "Our library hosted Rick Bragg not long ago, and he has got to be one of the best storytellers I've ever heard."

Aarene took this technique to high art in the following booktalk for teens.

📖 *The Worst Case Survival Handbook: Travel* by Joshua Piven, David Borgenicht, and David Cocannon

> During the summer weekends when I'm not busy being a librarian, I drive my horses around the state for racing competitions. I drive a twenty-seven-foot motorhome pulling a twenty-foot, fully loaded, three-horse trailer with two friends and three horses on board. The rig is nearly fifty-feet long including the hitch (about twice as long as the average classroom) and hinged in the middle.

One weekend, we were returning home after a very hot ride—ninety-seven degrees during the ten and a half hours of competition and no shade for most of the time. The temperature was down to about ninety-five when we pulled out and headed down the mountain road toward home. It was very hot. The road was steep, with a six-percent grade for eleven miles. At mile ten, the brakes glazed and failed. There was no shoulder and lots of oncoming traffic. There was a rock wall on our right side, and a thousand-foot cliff dropping off to the left. And we were still heading downhill with no brakes at all.

Fortunately, I had read *The Worst Case Scenario Survival Handbook*! In this book about travel, the authors give step-by-step instructions for an emergency stop with no brakes.

In case you ever need to know, this is what to do: Don't panic. Keep breathing! Shift into the lowest gear available and let the transmission slow you down. If there is room, "tack" back and forth across the road to slow down. Pump the brakes. It may not help, but it won't hurt, and you might be able to build up enough pressure to get some partial braking. Pull the emergency brake. This will cause the vehicle to turn sharply. (*Hint:* don't do this when towing a trailer or it may flip over!) Drive. You can steer around corners at much higher speeds than you normally do. Look for something to run into. A rock or cliff is a bad choice; a small tree (which will bend, break, and slow you down) is a better choice. Try not to run into another car. If you *must* drive off a cliff, try to go through the guardrail (or at least a bunch of trees) so that rescue workers will know where to begin looking for you.

I did all this (except drive off a cliff!), and finally the road sloped up a bit. I jammed the rig into park and hyperventilated for at least five minutes. Then we got out and directed traffic until someone was able to send us some help.

Now that I know all this stuff, I'll never forget the process of stopping with no brakes. But what if I ever get stuck in quicksand? Or abducted by aliens? Or have to stop a runaway camel? No worries—the *Worst Case Scenario* books have help for those situations too—and the books are small enough to take with you for use in any situation!

Booktalk by Aarene Storms. Reprinted with the permission of the author.

Aarene figures this must be the ultimate booktalk for this book, and I agree. She also told me to get my brakes checked.

Time to Refine

After you've written your booktalk, read your rough draft aloud. Is it longer or shorter than you expected? Have you included enough build up for your hook? Or maybe you included some extraneous action that needs to be cut. Are there any awkward phrases or words you consistently stumble over? Time how long it takes you to read it.

Now it's time to edit. Add or streamline as necessary. Make sure what you've written is true to your normal speech patterns, otherwise you'll feel awkward and sound unnatural. Read your booktalk aloud again. Does it have a natural flow to it? Does it feel easy in your mouth? Edit again if necessary.

One of the things that I love about listening to other booktalkers is how their booktalks always sound like them. Kirsten's energetic booktalks reflect her energetic approach to life. Holly's eloquent phrasing turns up in her booktalks, and Joy's humor always surfaces. You could gather a dozen booktalkers together to booktalk the same book, and you'd have a dozen different booktalks—in approach, content and style. It's a wonderful thing. Don't hesitate to make your booktalk your own.

Practicing your booktalk is the last step. Your own circumstances will dictate how you can best do this. Perhaps you have a tolerant partner, or pet, to whom you can deliver your booktalk. Maybe your children will be your audience. Be warned though that feedback from people who are related to you tends to be too generous or too critical. I personally prefer an empty room, walking path, or car. What you're after here is familiarity and ease of delivery. Don't worry about the "hows" of delivery yet, just work on the "what." Get the content fixed in your mind and the words to flow.

How Long Should My Booktalk Be?

How long an individual booktalk is really depends upon what you've chosen for your hook and how long a lead in you need to get there. It can be thirty seconds or five minutes. Rarely is a booktalk longer than that. Include some of each in your booktalking presentations. The length of an individual booktalk is really not as important as the structure. Get the structure right, and the length will take care of itself.

Having said that, let me make a comment on really long booktalks. I chatted with a library school student recently whose assignment was to booktalk two books for half an hour. I was stunned. Talking about a book for fifteen minutes, as she would have to do, is totally out of the realm of booktalking. You would have to give so much information about the book, reveal so much to fill that much time that you are no longer enticing, you're retelling or reviewing. It's a big difference.

Here's an example of a longer booktalk that focuses on a particular scene to introduce a character:

📖 *Walking Across Egypt* by Clyde Edgerton

Walking across Egypt is a novel, and despite the title, it doesn't have a thing to do with Egypt or even walking. *Walking Across Egypt* is the title of Mattie Rigsbee's favorite hymn and if you'd like to sing it, the music is right here in the book. Mattie Rigsbee is seventy-eight years old, and if you asked her, she'd tell you she was slowing down. Oh, she still lives by herself in her neat little brick house in her small North Carolina town. She still does all her own yard work and cooks all of her own meals, but she knows she's slowing down. That's why, when the stray dog shows up in her backyard, she calls the dogcatcher. "I can't be messing with a dog at my age," she said to herself and then went about her project for the day.

Because she's slowing down, Mattie decides to change the fabric on her kitchen chairs so she'll have something that's easier to wipe down. So she calls Bill Yeats, who does odd jobs for her, and tells him to come on out and pick up her chairs to redo. She tells him to come around lunchtime, and she'll fix him a little something to eat. Of course, by the time Bill shows up, Mattie has gotten busy with the screwdriver and has all the kitchen chair bottoms taken out. She's also added the bottom of her favorite rocking chair in the living room. After lunch, which wasn't much, just fried chicken, corn, potatoes, and home grown tomatoes, Bill takes off with the chairs.

Now Mattie has a secret vice, something that would purely humiliate her if her neighbors or any of the folk at church found out about. There was a particular soap opera that she likes to watch in the afternoon—and sometimes, she doesn't even wash her lunch dishes first.

This is one of those days when Mattie lets her dishes go and heads in to watch her program. She plunks herself down in her favorite rocking chair, completely forgetting that she has just sent off the seat to be recovered. Well, Mattie tries to heave herself out of the chair, but she can't move. She tries to tip herself over so she can crawl out, but she can't do that either. Mattie is just plain stuck, legs up in the air, watching the television from between her knees.

Finally, late that afternoon, Mattie hears a voice on the porch. It's Lamar Benfield, the dogcatcher. Stepping through the screen door, Lamar can see Mattie's predicament. "Ma'am," he says, "Can I help you?" "Oh, yes!" Mattie replies, her voice quavering with relief. "Would you go into the kitchen and do my dishes?" He does and then turns his attention to getting Mattie out of her rocking chair. It turns out that Mattie is well and truly stuck, nothing they try gets her out of that chair.

"Ma'am," Lamar says. I'm going to have to cut you out of that chair. Mattie is not the least bit in favor of this tactic. It's her favorite rocking chair, after all. But Lamar assures her that he's handy with wood and will take it home for repair so it will be just like new. Mattie agrees.

Lamar is as good as his word and brings back her rocking chair in fine shape. As they got better acquainted, Mattie discovers that Lamar has a nephew, Wesley, who is in the Young Men's Rehabilitation Center for stealing a car. For some reason, Wesley and his predicament hold some fascination for Mattie. She keeps thinking about what Jesus said about doing for the least of his brethren being the same as doing for him and Wesley certainly seems to be in the "least of my brethren" category.

Mattie decides to visit Wesley at the Young Men's Rehabilitation Center. She takes along a little something to eat—a hunk of her homemade pound cake, a huge wedge of apple pie, and some iced tea. Wesley is stunned, both by Mattie and the food. It's the best pie and cake he's ever tasted, but he can't figure out why this stranger would visit him. "Are you my grandma?" Wesley keeps asking.

One day, with memories of Mattie's cooking fresh in his mind, Wesley turns up on Mattie's doorstep. He tells her he is on leave from the rehabilitation center; could he have a little something to eat? Mattie takes a good look at Wesley and makes some interesting decisions. *Walking Across Egypt* by Clyde Edgerton.

You might never choose to do a booktalk this long, and that's perfectly fine. This isn't a booktalk that I do all the time, nor do I have many booktalks in my repertoire that are this long. I most often choose to do this booktalk with an audience for whom the storytelling aspect of the booktalk is of equal value to the actual recommendations. Some audiences, often those in retirement centers, just like to hear me tell the story, and this kind of a talk is well received. This storytelling quality is reinforced when I use a phrase like "slowing down" repeatedly. In everything from "The Three Little Pigs" to *King Lear,* three is that magic, mythic number in telling tales. In Mattie's case, the repetition becomes a sly joke that the audience enjoys. It's perfectly obvious to them that Mattie is nowhere near slowing down, even though she says she is. Seniors find this particularly piquant. On the other hand, businesspeople who are getting ready to bolt back to work after your presentation are not as likely to relax into this talk. With whatever audience you choose to use a longer booktalk, be sure that you surround it with shorter, snappier booktalks. You want your pace and delivery to be varied and lively, not long and droning.

Choosing Your Voice

I most often booktalk as myself telling about the characters because that's what I'm comfortable with. I generally only take on the voice of one of the characters if I'm reading from the book. You can, however, build and deliver the booktalk as if you were one of the characters in the book. Many young adult librarians do this with great results. Here are some samples of this kind of booktalk.

📖 *Speak* by Laurie Halse Anderson

I don't know why I called 911 at that August "back-to-school" party. I didn't mean to shut the party down or get all those kids taken in for underage drinking. Why does everyone assume I did it on purpose? Even my friends from middle school won't talk to me, sit near me, or have anything to do with me. Even my ex–best friend Rachel hasn't tried to find out why I did it. She just pretends I'm not there.

I never thought being in a crowd could be so lonely, but when I walk into the school cafeteria for lunch, I don't even know where to sit. There's not a single welcoming table. No one wants me. If I could just disappear altogether, I'd be happy—or at least not so depressed. Maybe there's a closet somewhere I can hide in.

And why is this senior football player, Andy Evans, bugging me? Where does he seem to know me from? It's not like we travel in the same social circles. Like I have a social circle. Ha. Ha. I've heard he's asked Rachel to the spring prom, but why do I feel that has something to do with me? Can't I just stay in my closet? Or will I finally have to SPEAK.

Read *Speak* by Laurie Halse Anderson

Booktalk by Peg Dombek. Reprinted with permission of the author.

📖 *Mary, Bloody Mary* by Caroline Meyer

By the time I was ten, I had grown so much like him that what happened changed my life forever. I had his fair skin, his blue eyes, and his shining red-gold hair. I even had his fiery temper. Oh, I loved my father so much. In my eyes King Henry was the handsomest man in the world, and I was his "perfect pearl," the Princess of Wales, first in line for succession to the throne. But all this changed when I turned eleven. For shortly after my birthday, Anne Boleyn came to court. With her dark beauty and clever wit, she beguiled my father. She turned him against my mother and led him to abandon me. Because of this evil woman who called herself queen, I almost lost my life. And for these crimes, Anne Boleyn deserved to die.

You think me cruel! You think me unjust! Well before judging me come and hear my story. I lost everything, my position, my honor, my mother's companionship, and my father's love. But I have survived, and now with my father's murderous behavior as the model, I am determined to be queen. I am *Mary, Bloody Mary* by Caroline Meyer.

Booktalk by Tom Reynolds. Reprinted with permission of the author.

📖 *Holes* by Louis Sachar

Imagine that you are Stanley Yelnatz, and every evening when you were growing up, you heard your father sing this lullaby:

> If only, if only the woodpecker cries
> The bark on the trees was as soft as the skies
> And the wolf howls below, so lonely, so lonely,
> If only, if only . . .

[*Change your stance: You are now Stanley Yelnatz*]

If only! If only those sneakers hadn'ta fallen outta da sky! If only I'dda left 'em alone. Howsz' I supposta know they were stolen? Do I look like the kind of person who'd steal from a charity auction?

[*Muttered sotto voce*] Don't answer that!

If only when the judge said I hadda choice between juvenile detention and Camp Greenlake, I hadn'ta chosen the camp! Howsz' I supposta know what it really was? I'd never been to summer camp? How bad could it be?

Bad. Real bad. I'm in boot camp with a lot of serious criminals. Murderers maybe! Out in the middle of the desert (Lake, hah!) with poisonous snake and lizards and scorpions. And y'know what they make us do? You're never gonna get this: They make us dig holes. Holes! Everyday you gotta dig a hole five feet deep and five feet wide all around. You don't get to eat or sleep or nothin' until you dig that stupid hole.

And it's all the fault of my no-good, rotten, pig-stealing great-grandfather. If he'd of kept his promise, then that old Gypsy lady would never've cursed us. Uh uh. And I wouldn't have such lousy luck. It's bad here. Crazy. I don't think I'm gonna survive this . . .

[*Return to being "the Narrator"*] Oh yeah, Stanley Yelnatz's life is going to get crazier than he knows. He thinks they're just making the prisoners dig holes to hurt them, maybe to break their spirit. But the holes are really linked to a secret and a murder and a curse. And Stanley? Why he's right, shall we say, dead in the center of it all. Oh yeah, Stanley is doomed!

Booktalk by Kirsten Edwards. Reprinted with the permission of the author.

> *[Kirsten's note to nitpickers: To be "doomed" is an old Anglo-Saxon word meaning to have a special fate. These guys being what they were, this naturally was assumed to be unpleasant.]*

If this is something that intrigues you and you feel comfortable with it, then try it out. It's a technique that you have to commit to totally, though. If you feel silly or self-conscious doing it, then it just won't carry.

Reading Aloud in Your Booktalk

Every once in awhile I find a book that speaks for itself much better than I ever could in giving the audience the flavor and tone of the book. Generally they are books where the writing style or the character's voice is particularly compelling. In these cases, I like to read aloud, briefly, from the book.

I will warn you from the outset that reading aloud from a book is an enterprise fraught with peril. I have heard many, many a booktalker read aloud from a book and few do it successfully. Too often, booktalkers turn into droners when they read aloud. The excitement and enthusiasm is absent, and it becomes snooze time for the audience. So I always caution my students to think long and hard about reading aloud.

On the other hand, I love to read aloud. There's nothing I like better than to let the faint suggestion of a Cajun accent slide into my voice as I read the first few paragraphs from Ken Wells's *Meely LaBauve*. Meely has such a wonderful, unique voice I just have to let him speak for himself. But I always pray fervently that no one who has even visited Louisiana is in my Pacific Northwest audience to critique my southern vowels. Likewise, I can't improve upon Esme Raji Codell's funny vignettes and sassy tone in *Educating Esme* or the precocious, brassy letters of Joey Margolis in *The Last Days of Summer* by Steve Kluger.

The key to reading aloud, if you choose to do it, is to pick a vivid passage and really become that character. Mary had just such an experience:

I was reading the short story "Bony Fingers" from the book *Scary Story Reader* when the "monster" character possessed me, and I started reading that character's lines in a voice I had not practiced. It made the story more effective, but it was unintentional!"

You see what can happen when you really get into your booktalk?

It's important to choose active passages full of the character's voice or the story's action. Do not choose long passages of scenic description, no matter how poetic it seems to you. Keep it just as lively as you can and avoid the read-aloud drone or what my friend Harvey calls "the beauty of it all syndrome." Don't softly read and expect the audience to come to you—they'll nod off. Jack it up several notches and go to them. Really show them the characters, the words that you're so taken with.

Using the Booktalks of Others

Librarians and teachers, generous souls that they are, are quick to share the booktalks that they've written. Joni Bodart, among others (see the list at the end of this chapter), has gathered together booktalks written by talented librarians that are yours for the taking. Why, you may ask, should I kill myself trying to write my own booktalks when I can just use someone else's? Tempting as it is, I implore you to resist. Your booktalk is your genuine excitement and enthusiasm about a book transmitted to your audience. To be most effective, it needs to be your own emotions and your own words. If I sound like a snotty purist, so be it, but please, I beseech you, write your own booktalks.

Now this is not to say that you shouldn't make use of these wonderful resources. You absolutely should. If you're just beginning and still trying to get the idea of what a booktalk looks, sounds, and feels like, these volumes are a great place to look, especially if you have no one in your community to observe. These books are also a great place to get ideas for books that are booktalkable. Cruise through them to get an idea of the characteristics that lend themselves to a great booktalk.

I also give you dispensation to use these sources if you've tried and tried to write a booktalk for a book you are sure is a winner but you just can't make work. Then reading or hearing someone else's booktalk can be a revelation. You know those, "Why on earth didn't I think of that?" moments. In those cases, feel free to borrow as long as you truly make it your own. Use the approach or the hook but make the language comfortable in your own mouth.

Biography of a Booktalk

If a booktalk doesn't come to you right away, don't worry about it. Booktalks rarely spring forth perfectly formed from the loins of Zeus. (I know, I know, it's really the head of Zeus.) Let it simmer for a while in your mind, or try out different approaches. Here's what happened to me with one book.

Practically from the first chapter of *Lying Awake* by Mark Salzman I knew it would be a great booktalk. The premise is unbeatable. Sister John of the Cross is a Carmelite nun who writes best-selling poetry based on visions in which she communicates with God. It turns out that her visions are epileptic seizures caused by a small tumor above her ear—easily removed by surgery. But if she chooses surgery, will she lose her visions and her poetry?

I was moved to tears by the scene in which Sister John began a night-long vigil in the chapel, trying to make this crucial decision about her health and the will of God. Soon all the sisters in the convent had joined her in silent support. When I described it to my husband, I started sobbing all over again. "Honey," he said, "if you're going to booktalk that book, it's going to take some work." Wise guy.

Sister John's decision is the obvious hook, so I started building the introduction to that point. I described her background as a contemplative nun, the importance of the visions to her spiritual life, and the importance of the income from her poetry to the order. Then I zoom in to more detail as she is diagnosed and must make her decision. What will it be?

It's really enough to give the true flavor of this book, but I really wanted to include the touching scene in the chapel, so I added it after the hook to flesh out the mood. Or so I thought.

My description of the scene went something like this:

"Sister John had asked for some time to make a decision about the surgery. Still unresolved, she began an all-night vigil in the convent chapel. On her knees after many hours, she was discouraged and about to give up. Then she felt a presence behind her; it was Mother Mary Joseph. As suddenly as she had appeared, Mother Mary Joseph vanished, and a short time later, all of the nuns filed into the chapel to hold vigil with Sister John."

So the first time I delivered this booktalk was to a small book club in a private home, always a more informal atmosphere. As soon as Sister Mary Joseph vanished, one of the women blurted out, "Where did she go? Did she just vanish into thin air?" Mood gone, game over. My sweet supportive nun had turned into a space traveler. "Beam me up, Scottie!" I tried a couple of more times with other groups before I finally admitted to myself that this scene is extraneous. Not only is it not necessary to the booktalk, it bogs it down and makes it more difficult to close. I would just have to content myself that readers would find this scene and enjoy it on their own. The other thing I discovered the first few times I did this booktalk is that I just can't easily say epileptic seizure, my tongue just can't consistently get around it, so rather than stumble over the phrase each time, or worry about stumbling over it each time, I eliminated it from the final rendition. I went back to the basics and now have a clean and pretty effective booktalk:

📖 *Lying Awake* by Mark Salzman

Sister John of the Cross had been a Carmelite nun for nearly thirty years. Her convent was set in a little piece of Eden surrounded by the freeways of urban Los Angeles. There had been long years when she wondered if hers was a true calling. Was hers a life of contemplative spirituality, or just drudgery? And then her visions began. They were clear, luminous, thrilling visions in which she felt that she was in direct communication with God. And when each vision was over, she was moved to write poetry, best-selling poetry that had become the major support of her order. Lately she had begun having severe headaches after her visions, but she didn't complain. She felt that if that was what it took to have such a rewarding personal relationship with God, then she was willing to pay the price. But one day, Sister John collapsed during prayers, and her mother superior insisted that she see a doctor.

"I have great news," the doctor said, after examining her test results. "Your seizures are caused by epilepsy brought on by a small tumor just above your ear. I can remove that tumor easily and you'll be as good as new." Sister John was stunned. Could it be that her rewarding spiritual life was manufactured by a physical cause? And if she chose to be cured, would she also lose her beautiful visions, her link with God?

It was a decision only Sister John could make. *Lying Awake* by Mark Salzman.

Additional Reading

📖 Bodart, Joni. *Booktalk! 2: Booktalking for all ages and audiences*, second edition. New York: H.W. Wilson, 1985.

Advice on how to write and deliver a booktalk plus sample booktalks. There are five volumes to choose from, but this one has the most information on technique.

📖 Bodart, Joni Richards, editor. *The Booktalkers' Companion: Volume I*. Denver, Colo.: BookHooks, 1994.

Booktalks plus a great article on the ABCs of booktalking by Patrick Jones.

📖 Bromann, Jennifer. *Booktalking That Works*. 2001. New York: Neal-Schuman.

Information about booktalking methods and sample booktalks.

📖 Jones, Patrick. *Connecting Young Adults and Libraries: A How to Do It Manual*, second edition. New York: Neal-Schuman, 1998.

Patrick clearly lays out the mechanics of booktalking in the chapter "Booktalking: Don't Tell, Sell."

📖 Littlejohn, Carol. *Keep Talking That Book!: Booktalks to Promote Reading, Volume II*. Worthington, Ohio: Linworth, 2000.

Brief booktalks on a wide range of books "for ages 8 to 80" arranged in order by author.

📖 MacDonald, Margaret Read. *The Storyteller's Start-up Book: Finding, Learning, Performing and Using Folktales*. Little Rock, Ark.: August House, 1993.

Check out the chapter "Learning the Story in One Hour" for techniques on remembering your booktalk.

📖 Schall, Lucy. *Booktalks Plus: Motivating Teens to Read*. Englewood, Colo.: Libraries Unlimited, 2001.

Booktalks grouped in topics relating to curriculum and to adolescent developmental tasks. Includes a summary of the book and related activities.

Stand Up and Sing Out! Delivering a Dazzling Booktalk

Now that you've got the structure down and a feeling for the words that you want to use, let's talk about presentation. This is where good booktalkers become great booktalkers by taking care in the way they deliver their message.

To Memorize or Not to Memorize

The fabled Margaret Edwards, author of *The Fair Garden and the Swarm of Beasts,* a classic book on service to young adults in the public library, held sway at the Enoch Pratt Library in Baltimore from 1932 to 1962. Legend has it that young adult librarians at Enoch Pratt Library under Ms. Edwards's reign memorized, word for word, a set number of standard booktalks before they were ever let loose on young adults. This is certainly one approach, and an admirable one. I can see the advantages of consistency and confidence building, especially in a large corps of young librarians who might not be experienced in booktalking. Certainly memorizing a script word for word is one way to go, but it does have its drawbacks. For one, you have to be comfortable with, and adept at, memorizing; not everyone is. Just the thought of memorizing dozens of booktalks verbatim would likely postpone my booktalking career indefinitely. It just sounds like work to me. But it might make you feel more prepared and therefore more comfortable.

Another thing to consider is if you memorize your booktalk, does your delivery sound canned? Are you able to inject fresh enthusiasm into the same words each time and not sound like you're singing the ABC song? This may not be an issue at all. You may find that when you don't have to worry about what to say next, your delivery is much smoother than it otherwise would be, that you can put all of your energy into how you're saying it rather than what you're saying.

The other thing about memorization is that terrifying question, "What happens if I forget?" It's a good question. What does happen if you forget? Will you be "Up there," as my favorite theatre director so colorfully says, "peeing in a fine mist?" Storytelling techniques are great for memorized work and standard storytelling technique for "going south" is to stop, breathe, and calmly wait for your thread to come back to you. Don't, don't, don't fluster and say you're sorry and you lost your place or anything of the kind. Just maintain eye contact and wait. Your audience won't know it's anything but a pause.

Here's a story my husband tells on himself. Many years ago, he went with a group of amateur actors to give a reader's theatre performance at a Job Corps camp. To begin the program, each actor stepped forward and introduced himself. When it was his turn, Will stepped forward, looked at the waiting audience, and paused. He couldn't remember his name. He says he doesn't remember being terrified or even particularly nervous, he just couldn't remember his name. He calmly turned around to his fellow actors and asked what his name was. As you might guess, they were somewhat incredulous, and it took him a moment or two to convince them that he really needed to know. In the end they told him, and he turned and introduced himself to the audience. Everyone had a good laugh, and nobody died of mortification or any other cause. The show went on without a hitch, and Will has had a great story to tell for twenty-five years.

You also need to think about the role of audience participation in your booktalks should you choose to memorize them. It's a booktalker's dream (or at least this booktalker's dream) to have a quiet, rapt audience, but that isn't always the case, especially if you are booktalking to children or teens. If you are working off a memorized script consider if interjected comments and questions will throw you off track. Maybe it's just the opposite, maybe having a solid script will keep you on track, less likely to digress or lose your place with "crowd interference."

To memorize or not to memorize? It's a personal decision. Here's my advice. If memorizing your booktalk sounds appealing to you, then try it. Start with one booktalk and memorize it. Try it out on several audiences and see how it goes.

Alternatively, if memorizing your booktalks sounds appalling to you, try it. Memorizing one booktalk won't kill you, and it will give you some additional experience and insight. Once you've done it a few times, you can vow never to do it again if it doesn't work for you. I think it's a good technique to have under your belt, even if you don't choose to use it all the time.

Maybe you'll want to split the difference, memorizing certain key parts of your booktalk and being more spontaneous with the rest of it. That's okay, too. The truth is, if you'll be booktalking frequently, this will become a moot point. The more you give a particular booktalk, the more it will settle in you mind, and the more you'll use particular phrases and emphases.

What to Do If You Don't Memorize

So if I write out my booktalks but don't memorize the whole thing, what do I do? Remember that giving a booktalk is, in effect, telling a story. So I recommend using another old storytelling technique, visualizing the story. After you finished writing out your booktalk, your story, put it away. Now close your eyes and picture in your mind the sequence of events that you've just written. Don't formulate words, just use pictures. Watch what unfolds. Do this several times. Memorize the plot of your booktalk. Once you have these images in your head, you'll always have the gist of the booktalk, whatever words you use. I find that with the kinesthetic act of writing, reading what I've written, and then visualizing it, all the learning styles have been covered; the booktalk is pretty well planted in my brain.

I once saw the radio program *A Prairie Home Companion* live. The highlight of the show, of course, is when Garrison Keillor, a storyteller par excellence, tells "the news from Lake Woebegone." As I watched and listened, Keillor paced around the stage without any notes, often with his eyes closed or with his back to the audience. It was for all the world like he was watching the movie in his head unfold and telling us about it. The words just flowed. All of us in the audience were hanging on every word. That's just the kind of fluid delivery I want for you. Concentrate on securing the story, and the words will follow.

Reading Aloud

If you plan to read aloud in one of your booktalks, make sure you go over those passages ahead of time. If you don't want to make notes on your book (I'm a librarian, I just can't do that), make a photocopy. Now read it aloud and pay attention as you read. Do you run out of breath before the end of a sentence? Are the dramatic spots getting the attention they deserve? Do you need to pause to build tension? It's helpful to go through and mark where to take a breath. That way, you get a breath when you need one, and the text will have a dramatic pause when it needs one. Give yourself plenty of time and plenty of breath. You don't need to race through your booktalk. By taking your time, you won't be tempted to run on and lose your breath. When you lose your breath, you lose your volume and your audience won't be able to hear you.

Now let's work on getting the words out of your mouth and into the ears of your eager audience. Here are some tips for delivering your booktalks that will help you be a potent performer.

Warm Up

Any actor or singer will tell you how important it is to warm up your voice. This is a gift you give yourself, a way of oiling the cogs of your presentation. It need not be elaborate. You don't need a special room or equipment, you just need to get your voice and body ready. Find some tongue twisters to say aloud and do some easy stretches. Breathe. You can easily do this in your car on the way to the booktalk (well, maybe not the stretches) or while taking a brief stroll after you arrive. If you have your room to yourself for a few minutes you can warm up there. Before you dismiss this as something you'd feel silly and self-conscious doing, give it a try.

The author Joni Rodgers taught me a good lesson about warming up. We were in my car on our way to one of our community libraries, where she was to give a talk. Joni had already done a couple of television interviews that morning, but being a conscientious performer, and a trained actor, she warmed up, in the car, on the way to the branch. She went through her vocal and breathing exercises, much as you might expect an opera singer to do, drilling syllables from soft to loud and back again and practicing tongue twisters. An actor warming up can be loud. An actor warming up in a small-ish car can be really loud. I was impressed—and temporarily a little deaf. When we got to the library, she took a few moments to herself in the restroom and then came out, started off her presentation with a song, and thoroughly delighted her audience.

Joni's actions reminded me that just because you are not speaking to several thousand people at Carnegie Hall doesn't mean your audience doesn't deserve your best. Warm up. You'll feel better and perform better, I promise.

Stand Up

Remember when your mother used to tell you to stand up straight and to speak up? Well, she was right. And it is truly amazing how many people never listened to their mothers.

The single most common mistake I see in booktalking or any other kind of public speaking is not standing still. I have heard speakers of all stripes from corporate bigwigs to agency trainers to authors. They may have a great story with a fabulous message, an engaging personality and a terrific speaking voice, but it's all lost if they don't stand still. I've seen some do a little box step in place—forward, sideways, back; forward, sideways, back. Now that's not presentation technique, that's how my mother taught me to dance when I was twelve. In a ballroom, fine, in front on an audience, no. I've seen others, in an effort to work two sides of a room, pace in a little aimless half moon. I worry for them. Where is it they want to go? Will they get there? Will they ever stop? So if you do nothing else in your booktalk, stand still. Your body will work better for you if you have your weight planted on your two feet.

Stand up right now. Straighten your spine. Lift your chin. Relax your arms and shoulders. (A friend tells me she always remembers a dance instructor's advice to "put your shoulders in your back pocket"). Now breathe. Focus your thoughts on what you want to say. Look at your imaginary audience. Now you are calm, focused, prepared, and powerful. Every time you waltz around in meaningless motions, you distract your audience from your message and lose that power.

You are communicating with your voice, your eyes, and your body language; let those shine through. Classic storytelling technique calls for little movement, few gestures. It's all done with the voice, the eyes, and facial expression. This is a good foundation for booktalking as well. Embroider later if you want to, but start with the basics.

Years ago I did a play in a community theatre that required me to do a monologue that was several pages long. I was alone on stage playing the role of a social worker who was delivering bad news to a couple who wanted to adopt a child. For that scene the playwright had cast the audience as the couple, and I was speaking directly to them. I wrestled and wrestled with how to do this scene effectively. Finally, I abandoned "acting" and called up all of my storytelling skills. I sat quietly with no hand gestures at all and just told the story with as much intensity and focus as I could muster, directing my gaze deliberately throughout the auditorium where the audience would be. The director (finally) was delighted. "That's it!" he said. "Tonight you had real presence." I was so delighted myself that I later married the director. You see what focus can do for you?

Watch speakers and see for yourself what's most effective. Watch politicians giving a speech. They are planted, aren't they? They don't wander around; they stand still and project.

I can practically hear you sputtering, "What about animation and movement? Aren't those good things? I've seen lots of good speakers and storytellers moving around and gesturing!" In the first place, don't mistake animation for movement. They aren't the same thing. Animation can come from the vibrancy in your voice, the twinkle in your eye and the enthusiasm you portray. It doesn't come from manic movement around the room.

There is absolutely a place for movement and for gestures, but these things are built on a solid, powerful anchor, and they are deliberate, not aimless or random. The next time you go to professional theatre, watch the actors move. They don't wander across the stage, making you wonder where they are going and why. They move from one point on the stage to another point with deliberation, purpose, and energy. It's a clean movement with a definite start and a definite stop. It tells the audience that the actors know what they're doing and provides the trust and confidence the audience needs to go along with them.

Watch professional storytellers and stand-up comics. They use gestures carefully, as punctuation. Gestures come at just the right time and add rather than distract. For instruction on what not to do, you can watch nearly any car dealer or appliance merchant who does his own commercials. Whew! Some of those dudes could power small cities with the wind generated from their gestures. And then there are the lamentable speakers who favor the fig leaf pose with hands clasped demurely together somewhere in the vicinity of . . . well, you get the picture.

If you want to use movement, fine. But first, make sure you're working from a well-built foundation. Then think about it. Make sure it's appropriate. Make the gesture strong, sure, and clean, then stop. Don't flail. Don't be tentative. Keep your hands in front of you in the "neutral zone" between the hips and shoulders. And if I hear about you nervously jingling the change in your pocket while you're booktalking, I'm coming after you.

If you often work a large room you may feel that you have to move around to include everyone. This may be so. If that's truly the case, then do what you need to do with decision and authority. But first try this: swivel. Or try this: pivot. Our bodies are wondrous machines, and we are blessed with the capability to move our heads and upper torsos without necessarily moving our feet.

The second most common mistake I see in booktalking and other presentations is sitting. We seem to all have a common desire to be just folks, and we want to prop ourselves on a table while we're talking. I have two words and a contraction for you: don't do it! My library school students howl when I give them this advice. "But I'm just a casual sort of person," they cry. "I'm so much more comfortable sitting." Tough toenails. I'm all for your being comfortable, but I'm much more interested in your being mesmerizing. Sit down, and half your power is gone. You are saying, nonverbally, that what you have to tell me is not really important. You're making it harder on yourself to capture the attention of your audience, harder to breathe, harder to focus, harder to pull energy up and out. Don't put yourself under that handicap. Stand. The only exception to this that I can think of is if you're speaking to a small group in someone's living room and everyone is seated. In that case, choose the highest, straightest chair in the room and stay very erect.

I have had students who just had to sit to booktalk, despite my best advice to the contrary. And as soon as they sat, no matter how good my intentions, much of my attention was gone. They weren't commanding now, they were asking for sufferance. Pooh on that, I say. And then it often got worse. They'd be sitting on a table so cozily and comfortably that they'd begin to swing their legs. If they only had part of my attention before, they had all of it now. Unfortunately, it was all directed at their kneecaps or feet. Movement is a big punch, there is absolutely no way I can focus on what you're saying while I'm watching your legs swing back and forth. Talk about mesmerizing. What did they say? I have no idea. Save yourself and your audience from this unnecessary aggravation. Stand planted on your own two feet like the big person you are and speak out. Which leads us to the next tip.

Think Big

When you speak to a group, you need to amplify not only your voice but yourself. You need to be you in a larger, more intense way to fill the room and capture attention. Breathe deeply. Think big. Think about filling the space with your presence. Make it a conscious effort. Trainer extraordinaire Guila Muir advises imagining a circle of light that you step into, leaving personal woes and distractions behind. Think only about what you have to say and making a connection with your audience.

Speak Up

The best courtesy you can pay your audience is to speak loudly enough so that they can hear you. You know yourself how frustrating it is to be in an audience, perhaps for a speaker that you really wanted to hear, and only be able to hear parts of it. It's a situation that makes me furious. Recently a representative of an employee assistance agency addressed a group of managers for our library system. She had clearly dressed carefully for the occasion, projecting an image of knowledgeable professionalism. What she had to say was certainly germane, and for some staff, wildly important. However, she spoke so softly that we all had to strain to hear her. She was competing with the air-conditioning system in the room, the backchat of the audience, and the building construction across the street. Do I remember what she said? Alas, no. All of my energy went into trying to hear her—and then into being annoyed that she was making me work so hard. Unless you've got competition from road machinery or airplanes or maybe you're making an address to hundreds of thousands in front of the Lincoln Memorial on the Mall in Washington, D.C., there is absolutely no reason not to make yourself heard. It's okay to use a microphone if you need one, and some venues (like the Lincoln Memorial) demand one. But you'll be way ahead of the game if you can make yourself heard in ordinary circumstances. Be aware of it, and practice if you need to. Here are some pointers to help you.

Volume is all about breath. If you have breath, you can have volume. You don't have to yell, just put more breath behind what you're saying and you'll be louder. That's what actors and singers do. Just ask my friend Kathy Svajdlenka, singer and voice teacher. Here's advice from the diva.

Breathing

(Or, "How *Does* She *Do* That?")

Do you ever wonder how an opera singer manages to fill up a cavernous opera house with her voice, without the use of microphones? When an opera singer opens her mouth to begin an aria, she is using a set of learned muscle actions to take in and then propel air out of her body at a controlled speed. The stronger those muscle actions are, the clearer her vocal projection is. This is why a trained professional singer almost never needs to use a microphone to be heard in a large opera house.

Speaking in front of an audience is much like singing in front of an audience. In each case, you stand before a group of people to whom you communicate ideas through the use of your voice. Like singing, prepared speaking requires those same learned muscle actions that a singer uses to project to an audience.

Voice Anatomy 101

The average breath taken by the average person on an average day uses only about one-third of a person's lung capacity. That third constitutes the upper portion of the lungs and chest muscles. But watch a baby as it sleeps—you'll notice that her whole chest and abdomen move up and down with each inhalation and exhalation. Try it yourself. Lie on your back and relax. Notice how your breath moves lower in your body. Now, you are breathing with more of your lung capacity.

Our torso is filled with organs and muscles all working in cooperation with one another. The diaphragm, a large, flexible, dome-shaped sheet of muscle separating the lungs from the abdomen, is the major muscle controlling the breath. When you inhale, the diaphragm contracts, its dome shape flattening to allow the lungs to fill with oxygen. When you exhale, the diaphragm relaxes back up into its dome shape, forcing carbon dioxide out of the lungs. In our lying-at-rest breath, the diaphragm contracts, making space for the lungs to fill up with air; the abdomen is pushed down and out onto its own supportive set of muscles to accommodate the movement of the diaphragm.

Try it out. Pretend you are going to blow up a balloon. Hold the balloon to your lips and blow a steady stream of air into your imaginary balloon. Notice how your abdominal muscles contract. This contraction provides support for the diaphragm, allowing it to exert a steady flow of pressure against the lungs, pushing air out of them.

Allowing the abdomen to be pushed down and out by the diaphragm is what is known in the singer's world as a "belly out" breath. The portion of your abdomen beneath your ribs and above your belly button moves out each time you inhale. Try it. Place your palms on your abdomen, the portion under your rib cage and above your belly button. Middle fingers should just touch each other. Inhale, sipping your breath in as if through a straw in one long sip. As you intake your breath push out this portion of your abdomen, making a space between your middle fingers. Exhale and do it three more times. Feel the strength of these abdominal muscles as they support your intake of breath.

Which brings us to posture. Good posture is essential to good breath support. If the diaphragm, lungs, and abdomen are all working together to produce a full, supported breath, they need room to do their jobs. Posture that is not erect and relaxed will defeat any efforts at good breath support. Try it. Round your shoulders and slouch. Hunch your back so that your chest is pulled inward toward your spine. Now, try to breathe the way you have just learned above. Feel strong? Probably not. But now try this. Stand with your feet about shoulder width apart and stretch your arms way above your head. Slowly bring your arms down to your sides. You should feel expansiveness in your chest. Your shoulders will be naturally down and back, and you will be standing up tall and erect. Now, take your "belly out" breath. Feel strong? You bet!

Incidentally, breathing in this way not only provides you with the stamina you need to give a presentation or sing a song, it also quiets those nervous butterflies. The more oxygen your muscles and organs receive, the more supple and responsive they are. Feeling nervous is a "fight-or-flight" response that your body goes through when it is presented with a stressful situation. With more supple and fluid muscles, you will be able to "fight" as opposed to "flee" from your presentation.

The basic mechanics of supportive breathing are like any other physical activity that isn't done all the time. Just like dancing or playing baseball or running, the more you practice it, the easier and more automatic it becomes. Professional athletes don't have think about each move before they do it because they have done it for so long that they move without having to consciously think about how to place their bodies and move their muscles. The same goes for supportive breathing. Here are a few activities you can do to practice breath support.

Speak. Inhale a "belly out" breath and hold while reciting the Pledge of Allegiance on one breath. Run all the words together. Keep your abdomen out as long as you can (remember the "blowing up the balloon" feeling?). Your goal is to say the entire pledge on one breath.

Hiss. Inhale a "belly out" breath, hold and exhale on a hiss. Keep your abdomen out as long as you can, supporting that diaphragm. Time yourself to see how long you can go before you are completely out of air.

Sing. Inhale a "belly out" and hold, singing your favorite song in one long breath. Hold out your abdomen and run all the words together. Try it the next time you are singing along to the radio in your car.

Let your breath support work for you, and your next presentation will be a pleasure for both you and your audience.

Before you begin any presentation, do a sound check. Speak to your audience and ask if you can be heard. Watch and see if those heads are bobbing yes in the back row. Like I said before, if you need a microphone, use a microphone. If you are using a microphone, this is time to adjust it to a comfortable level. And for Pete's sake, adjust it, don't just toy with it ineffectually. Don't put up with it being at the wrong height because you don't know how to adjust it or don't want to bother. You are important enough to be heard, and this is a tool that will help you. If you can manage your toaster and your can opener, you can manage a microphone.

Maintain Eye Contact

Remember I said that you get your message across to an audience primarily through your voice and eyes? Studies show that if an audience remembers nothing else about a speaker, they remember eye contact. Let's talk about your eyes. In this kind of presentation, you're not talking to a group but to the individuals gathered together. This means you don't stare over the tops of heads at some point at the back of the room, you look at individuals. Facing a group, no matter how large or how small, pick out members of the audience and hold eye contact for just a second or two. Do this systematically, not randomly. I generally start to my right in the front row, hold the gaze of someone for a second, and then move to the second or third row and do the same thing. My eyes move, row by row, to the back of the room, then I begin in the back on the left side and move forward row by row. When I'm done I start on the right side again and pick different people and make eye contact. No, this doesn't look funny. My head doesn't necessarily even move a lot. My eyes move, make contact, and move on. This makes each member of the audience feel like I'm talking directly to them—and I am! Remember, a second or two is all it takes. If you stare fixedly at one person for much longer than that, the person will become uncomfortable and start to squirm.

If you absolutely come unglued by the thought of looking people in the eye, then cheat to start out with. Look at their eyebrows and it will have much the same effect. As you get more comfortable, you'll be able to look your audience members in the eye and make genuine contact.

Don't Let Stage Fright Scare You

Speaking of coming unglued, the most common question I get from my library school students when we talk about booktalking is about stage fright. "How can I not be so scared?" they ask me, and it's a question I've pondered a lot. If you're nervous about speaking in public, know that you're not alone. Statistics show that more people have a fear of public speaking than fear death. Yikes!

There's almost nothing I'd rather do than public speaking, but that doesn't mean that I don't get nervous. An actor friend once told me, "Nerves are your friends." They give you that extra boost, that extra energy that allows you to reach out to your audience. You are more aware of everything around you and your reflexes are sharper. There's a reason it's called nervous energy. Channel it into your booktalk.

When the author and actor Malachy McCourt visited our library system I was impressed with his absolute ease in front of an audience and his ability to speak off the cuff about just about anything. I had the opportunity to ask him about stage fright and what his advice would be to booktalkers. He replied that the most important thing was not to deny your fear. Malachy said that you should admit to yourself that you're frightened if you are, but at the same time reassure yourself that you are going to do the very best you can. I hadn't thought about it in just that way, but it's good advice. It doesn't make sense to spend your energy trying to talk yourself out of being frightened. Accept it and move on.

The actor and director Garry Marshall also had a thing or two to say about nerves in a television interview. (You know Garry Marshall, he played the chocolate king in the movie *A League of Their Own* and directed *The Princess Diaries*.) His advice for self-talk in a frightening situation (like directing a movie for the first time) sounded much like Malachy's. Say to yourself, "I'm nervous. This is a little scary. Now, concentrate!" (Of course, to get the full effect of this advice you have to imagine hearing Garry's broad New York accent.) If you make sure you are well prepared and warmed up, half the battle will be won. As for the rest, it might help to think of it this way. Booktalking isn't about you. It's about the books. Booktalking is a gift you give to friends you have yet to meet. And when were you last nervous about giving a gift to a friend?

Chance Hunt is a children's librarian now, but he was an actor in a former life, so he knows a thing or three about getting ready to perform. Here is Chance's best advice for getting ready to go on:

A Booktalker Prepares

I believe that if people giving a presentation can speak clearly, with confidence, and with focus, they will have a much better time (and do a better job) when speaking to a group. Warming up is something that helps you do just that. Preshow preparation is to help you relax, to get the body prepared for what it's going to do, to get creativity flowing, and to focus your mind so that you can communicate your passion for books and reading at your absolute best. Whether it's a five-minute or a thirty-minute warm-up, take the time you need to be ready to present.

Breathe

It all starts here. Without breath, you will have no voice. It is sound supported by the breath that allows the actor or singer to speak and sing without straining the vocal chords. Breath starts below the lungs and beneath the belly, not in the throat. Your body already knows this; it's just that our minds have gotten in the way. Practice this:

Relax your stomach—let it hang without sucking it in. Now, slowly contract or press in the stomach muscles (diaphragm) toward your spine. If you are doing it correctly, you should feel air pressing upward and out of your mouth. Once you have pressed all of the air out, relax your stomach again. Air will automatically come in and fill your belly. Don't suck in the air, but allow it to come back into your body. Do this a few times so that you can feel the connection between your diaphragm and your breath.

Next, as you are contracting the muscles, begin to speak—the alphabet is a good place to start. As you speak, let the breath continue out just as easily as when you were contracting and not speaking. When you run out of breath, relax your stomach muscles, let the breath fill you up, and begin speaking again. This is the first step to finding correct technique in properly connecting your breath with your voice. It is not a bad idea for those who will be doing a lot of public speaking to take a voice class.

Warm Up Your Tongue

Just as you stretch and warm up the muscles before going for a jog or playing a sport, warm up your speaking muscles before your talk. One big muscle that needs some warming up is your tongue, and a fun way to do it is with tongue twisters like the following:

- Rubber baby buggy bumpers
- A box of biscuits, a batch of mixed biscuits
- Six thick thistle sticks. Six thick thistles stick
- Red leather. Yellow leather.
- Unique New York and Kinky Cookie

These are short ones, but also good for getting your voice up in your nose a little bit, which helps with projection. You can find additional tongue twisters online at *http://www.geocities.com/Athens/8136/tonguetwisters.html*

Moisten Your Throat

Drink lots of water, and have water available to you for your talk. Moist vocal chords are happy vocal chords.

Pace Yourself

Don't use all of your energy and vocal stamina while talking about the first book. If you'll be talking for thirty minutes, or talking all day, make sure you are taking care of your voice by not blowing it all out in the first five minutes.

Know the Space

Allow some time to know where you'll be speaking. Whether it's a library meeting room or a public auditorium, you need to test out your voice and how the room feels ahead of time. If you'll be using a microphone, this will be time well spent, allowing you to get comfortable not only with the sound but also the limitations of the equipment you'll be using.

Take the Stage

There is a *big* difference between walking on and making an entrance. Making an entrance means exuding the confidence in yourself and the material you will be presenting. Be proud of yourself and what you know; don't slink on as if you need permission to be there. Be there from the beginning.

> **Stop to Focus**
>
> Along with getting to your destination, checking out the space ahead of time, warming up your tongue, and finding out where the bathroom is, make sure you take a couple of minutes before you start to *do nothing*. Focus your mind, your thoughts. Visualize what you are about to do (and being wonderful at it). Take three or four slow, deep breaths. Scrunch your shoulders up to your ears, and let them drop two or three times. Let your body relax, and let your mind focus.

You'll note that Chance and I agree about a number of presentation techniques. Smart guy, that Chance.

The Audience Reacts (or Maybe Not)

A fascinating and sometimes frustrating fact of booktalking is that every single audience you talk to will be different. Their level of attention will be different, the dynamic will be different, the mood in the room will be different, their reaction to you will be different. A booktalk that brought down the house in the seventh-grade class you talked to last period may elicit nothing but shrugs this period. Be prepared, be flexible, and be responsive. As long as you know anything can happen, you won't be quite so taken aback when it does.

My guess is that some of you are shrugging at me, thinking, "What's the big deal? Just let me give the booktalk. I'm not an actor. Leave me alone with all this petty presentation business." Presentation skills are what get you out of your own way and let your passion for your books shine through. Polish your presentation skills, and your audience won't be counting your "uhs," watching your waving kneecaps, or straining to hear you. They'll be fascinated by the stories your books have to tell. And isn't that what it's about?

Finding Help

The best way to be at ease in front of an audience is to practice. You will, I promise, become better and better the more you booktalk. You'll see how the audience reacts, and you'll be able to fine-tune your presentation. Nonetheless, a grounding in public speaking or a refresher in presentation skills is never a bad idea, especially if you're feeling a little nervous or self-conscious. Look around your community and see what's offered. There may be a basic speech class at the community college or a storytelling class offered by a library school or education department. As you can probably tell, I am a huge fan of storytelling techniques. I believe a background in storytelling can give you great presence and focus. If there is no class available, check online to see if there is a storytellers' guild in the area that you can join.

How about Toastmasters? There's an organization whose sole purpose if to help you improve your public-speaking abilities. To see if there's a group near you, contact Toastmasters International, P.O. Box 9052, Mission Viejo, CA 98690; Tel. (949) 858-8255; *www.toastmasters.org*

A beginning acting class can give you a great background for being in front of an audience and is particularly good for learning movement and voice production (otherwise known as volume). Failing that, is there a community theatre group in your town? Try out for a role, or work backstage and listen to what the director tells the actors. Watch and learn the exercises the actors do before a performance.

However you choose to improve your skills, give yourself tons of credit for making the effort. It's not an easy thing to face your fears or to wrestle with learning something as an adult, especially if it doesn't come easily (ask me about my piano lessons!). But it's an investment that will pay you back time and time again in increased comfort, ease, and joy.

Additional Reading

📕 Kahle, Peter V.T., and Melanie Workhoven. *Naked at the Podium: The Writer's Guide to Successful Readings*. Seattle, Wash.: 74th Street Productions, 2001.

A book for writers on tour promoting their own book, this volume has lots of helpful presentation hints for booktalkers as well.

📕 Linklater, Kristin. *Freeing the Natural Voice*. 1976. Hollywood, Calif.: Quite Specific Media Group (Drama Publishers), 1985.

One of the classic books on voice and breath, filled with lots of relaxation and focusing exercises.

📖 Lipman, Doug. *Improving Your Storytelling: Beyond the Basics for All Who Tell Stories in Work or Play*. Little Rock, Ark.: August House, 1999.

>   Good advice on how to learn a story, use your voice well, and overcome fear that booktalkers as well as storytellers can use.

📖 MacDonald, Margaret Read. *The Storyteller's Start-Up Book: Finding, Learning, Performing, and Using Folktales Including Twelve Tellable Tales*. Little Rock, Ark.: August House, 1993.

>   You'll find the chapter on "Performing the Story" applicable to booktalks as well.

📖 Ristad, Eloise. *A Soprano on Her Head: Right-Side-Up Reflections of Life and Other Performances*. Moab, Utah: Real People Press, 1982.

>   A wonderful blend of philosophy and pragmatism that will help you make your own rules for performing and for overcoming stage fright.

📖 Slutsky, Jeff, and Michael Aun. *The Toastmasters International Guide to Successful Speaking: Overcoming Your Fears, Winning Over Your Audience, Building Your Business and Career*. Chicago: Dearborn Financial, 1997.

>   Take a look at the chapter "Developing Your Gestures, Body Language, Voice Modulation, and Vocal Variety."

Booktalking to Adults

Booktalking to adults seems to get short shrift in the spectrum of library services these days. When you talk to avid, active booktalkers, they are most often involved in booktalking to children or teenagers. That's truly a shame because adults are as enthralled by and as much in need of the benefits booktalking can offer as kids are, perhaps more so. Unlike children and teens, most adults have the time constraints endemic in working and participating in family and community life. Booktalking is heaven sent for this group. It gives them a universe of books to choose from that they probably wouldn't otherwise hear about. If you give these folks an engaging booktalk about some lesser-known titles, you can free them from the shackles of the best-seller lists in the newspaper or the paperbacks displayed at the grocery store. All they need is your list of titles and a phone or computer, and they easily can add terrific books to their life. If your agency is not currently offering booktalks for adults as part of your services, consider it. I think you'll find the audience as responsive and the rewards as great as booktalking to young people.

Speaking of young people, Harry Potter may have been a wake-up call to many adults that there's children's literature out there that they should not miss. I love to include at least one children's book in my booktalks for adults. I tell them it's a special treat. After all, why should kids get all the good stuff? Adults love to have permission to enjoy children's books, especially when they don't have children at home. In addition to enjoying the books themselves, booktalking children's titles to adults gives them a glimpse into what's happening in that other literary world—and gives them great ideas for gifts and read-alouds for the special young people in their lives. Here are some thoughts about kids' books that you can booktalk to adults:

Not Just for Kids

Picture Books

📖 *CLICK, CLACK, MOO Cows That Type* by Doreen Cronin
Farmer Brown has a problem. His cows have found the old typewriter in the barn.

📖 *My Little Sister Ate One Hare* by Bill Grossman
There's just no telling what little sisters will do.

📖 *Olivia* by Ian Falconer
Nothing ever tires this pig out.

Just for Fun

📖 *The Abracadabra Kid* by Sid Fleischman (autobiography)
The autobiography of the Newbery award–winning children's author who set out from childhood to be a magician.

📖 *A Long Way from Chicago* by Richard Peck (fiction)
Joey and his younger sister Mary Alice travel to visit their unconventional grandmother every August from 1929 through 1935.

📖 *Save Queen of Sheba* by Louise Moeri (fiction)
After Indians attack their wagon train, King David must try to save himself and his sister, Queen of Sheba.

📖 *Time Stops for No Mouse* by Michael Hoeye (fiction)
Adventures ensue when watchmaker mouse Hermux Tantamoq meets dashing aviatrix Linka Perfliger.

📖 *Woodsong* by Gary Paulsen (memoir)
Award-winning children's author recounts his experiences learning to drive a dogsled.

Thought Provokers

📖 *Cool Women* by Dawn Chipman, Mari Florence, and Naomi Wax (nonfiction)
The thinking girl's guide to the hippest ladies in history, both real and imaginary, from Catwoman to Cleopatra.

📖 *Earthshine* by Theresa Nelson (fiction)
> Slim watches over her father, a disarmingly charismatic man, as his struggle with AIDS reaches its climax.

📖 *Let the Celebrations Begin!* by Margaret Wild (picture book)
> Concentration camp survivors prepare for the liberation.

📖 *Mind's Eye* by Paul Fleischman (fiction)
> Unlikely nursing home roommates sixteen-year-old Courtney and eighty-eight-year-old Elva take an imaginary journey together using a 1910 Baedeker's guide to Italy.

📖 *Missing May* by Cynthia Rylant (fiction)
> After being passed among relatives, Summer joins her aunt and uncle and marvels at the couple's deep love for one another. But after Aunt May dies, Summer and Uncle Ob are brought together in their struggles to come to terms with her death.

When considering booktalking to adults, don't limit yourself to the obvious literary groups and books clubs. Of course, these are wonderful venues for your presentations, but there are many other adult groups that may be just as interested—women's groups, business groups, church groups, and so on. Brainstorm a list of possibilities, and then get to work.

I talked earlier about keying in to discrete groups in your community as audiences for your booktalking program. Here's how to find them, let them know about you, and decide what to booktalk when you get the engagement.

Booktalking to Seniors

Seniors are great audiences. They are a demographic group that votes, for one thing, if that's an issue for you. They generally have more leisure time so they are able to take part in group activities and listen to programs like yours. They grew up in an era that called for a greater development of attention span and listening skills, always a treat for a speaker. Not only that, there are lots of them. There are 78 million baby boomers in the United States, aging as you read this.

Finding Your Audience

The local senior center is the place to begin searching for this group. Call the director and explain the program you're offering. See if there are any book groups already going. If not, maybe you can help get one started. It's not that difficult to do a short session on how a book group can function, followed by booktalks and a list of potential book group titles; that may be all it takes to launch a group.

Check on the Internet to see if there is an association of school retirees in your community. They're active, they're organized, and they love to hear about books.

Retirement complexes are another great venue for reaching seniors. Look for facilities that offer a full slate of activities and that cater to busy, active folk. Large retirement complexes that have detached houses as well as apartment complexes are likely to have resident-run groups with which you can connect. Call the office and see where you might be able to fit in. Smaller facilities such as apartments generally have an activity director who will be delighted to hear from you. Call and introduce yourself and your program. Then follow up with a brief letter and your business card so that the activity director has all the information at hand when preparing the next month's schedule. You know how easy it is to forget about a phone call that's an interruption in a busy day. Write it down and send it off. Make it easy to remember. And if you don't get any results, follow up in a few months. There's often a high turnover in activity directors. The next one may be more receptive.

I'm lucky in that we have a large and active traveling library that visits many of the senior facilities in the county. They are good about giving my name to groups that may be interested in having me come to booktalk.

Choosing Your Books

I like to take at least a couple of titles that touch on periods of time or life experiences that the group may have had, and they seem to really enjoy hearing about books to which they can really relate. "Oh good! A book about somebody our age," is how one woman responded when I started talking about such a title. Doris Kearns Goodwin's book *Wait Till Next Year* is a great memoir about growing up in the forties and fifties, and it often sparks lively reminiscences about the arrival of that first television or long awaited new refrigerator in the post–WWII era. Once I talked about *Amelia Earhart's Daughters* by Leslie Haynsworth and David Toomey, an accounting of women's aviation during WWII, to a group of senior women. I discovered that one of them was a pilot who could tell plenty of great stories of her own.

Be wary of making too many assumptions about what this group will and won't like, especially in terms of literary merit or sexual content. Seniors have a rich background of life experiences that will surprise you if you think of everyone as a caricature of grandma or grandpa. We often think of older people as wanting "gentle reads" and old standards. In fact, the demand for Seifert, Hill, and Loring has fallen off, replaced by an interest in today's authors. This will become even more true as the baby boomers age. I was once introduced to a gentleman after a booktalk who turned out to be a retired book reviewer for the *New York Times*. I immediately wondered if I had included enough challenging books of literary merit.

My biggest lesson came when talking to a large group of seniors in a Christian retirement community. I included *Julie and Romeo* by Jeanne Ray, focusing on the fact that these two Boston florists came from families that hated each other for reasons no one remembered. I led up to the budding romance and the consternation of their children and the family mayhem that ensued. Then I talked about hearing the author speak. She discussed her frustration that women over fifty were written off by popular culture, and how this had led her to write the book. I shied away from talking about the physical relationship of the two main characters, nervous that such a thing would not go over well.

It was obvious from the nods and smiles during my talk on this book that several people had already read it. Imagine my surprise when one woman came up to me after the booktalk telling me how much she liked *Julie and Romeo* and how glad she was that I had talked about it. "But," she continued, "why didn't you talk about the part where they got caught naked in the refrigerator? That was such a funny scene." Why indeed? So much for prudish old poops. And so much for my preconceptions.

The next time I booktalked *Julie and Romeo* was to a group of women at a senior center. I gave them the same booktalk I had given before and then added that the prior group had wanted to know why I didn't include "the refrigerator scene." The ladies roared with laughter and referred to it several times while I was there. As I was packing up to leave, they were discussing which books they would read as a group. Heading out the door, the last words I heard were, "Let's start with that naked book!"

Special Considerations for Seniors

Your senior audience will appreciate it if you include titles that are also available in large print and audio formats. Large print publishers are a savvy group and have caught on to the changing demographics and the changing tastes of older readers so you can really find a wide range of titles available in this format.

When you booktalk to seniors, it's especially important to remember to keep your volume up. Most retirement facilities have a microphone set up as a matter of course, but for smaller groups, it might just be you and them. It's unfair to assume that all seniors have hearing problems, but we generally tend to lose some hearing acuity as we grow older, so it's a good bet that at least some of your audience has some hearing loss. Don't shout, just speak clearly and keep your breath going and your volume up.

Booktalking to seniors who just happen to live in a communal arrangement, such as a retirement apartment, is very different from talking to patients in assisted-care facilities or nursing homes. Because the range of functionality of the residents in care facilities is so wide, you are likely to find yourself in a role of entertainment rather than information (and sometimes even that's questionable). I once spoke at a senior residence that had many different levels of care. I didn't realize that I had been booked to speak to a group that was in the skilled care portion of the facility until I started the program. Their ability to attend and understand what I was saying was much less than a typical group, and to be understood I had to change dramatically what I said about the books and how I said it. At one point, as I scanned my audience to make that all-important eye contact, twelve out of the fifteen audience members were asleep! Here's where you need to review the goals for your booktalking program and see if this is the audience you're after.

The occasional snooze aside, booktalking to seniors is great fun. I've found seniors to be open to all sorts of books, but I always like to include one or two that either feature older protagonists or deal with a time period that is especially relevant to older adults. Here are some examples:

Booktalks for Seniors

📖 *All Over but the Shoutin'* by Rick Bragg (memoir)
> It's not necessarily journalist Rick Bragg that older adults relate to in this book, it's his affection for his mother and the hard times that she endured.

📖 *Amelia Earhart's Daughters* by Leslie Haynsworth and David Toomey (nonfiction)
> The section on women in aviation during World War II holds particular interest for seniors.

📖 *The Coalwood Way* by Homer Hickam (memoir)
> This sequel to *Rocket Boys* focuses on events in the town of Coalwood in 1959 while Homer and his friends are working on their rockets. Many older folks relate to this eloquent evocation of small-town life.

🕮 *Courting Emma Howe* by Margaret A. Robinson (fiction)
> There's just something about a western setting and a homesteading scenario that appeals across the generations.

🕮 *Ethel and Ernest: A True Story* by Raymond Briggs (nonfiction)
> The story of Briggs's parents' courtship and marriage, in graphic-novel format. Seniors appreciate the scope of the story and all of the changing times that the couple endured.

🕮 *The Greatest Generation* by Tom Brokaw.
> The personal stories of those who fought World War II, at home and abroad.

🕮 *Miss Julia Speaks Her Mind* by Ann B. Ross (fiction)
> Becoming independent after the death of a spouse is one of the themes older women can relate to in this book. They also appreciate the humor and spunk that Miss Julia Springer displays.

🕮 *Mountain City* by Gregory Martin (nonfiction/memoir)
> Seniors are intrigued by the concept of Greg Martin spending the summer working in his grandparent's store, observing a vanishing way of life in a small Nevada town.

🕮 *The Persian Pickle Club* by Sandra Dallas (mystery)
> The ladies of Harveyville, Kansas, find solace in their quilting society during the dust bowl years.

🕮 *The Pumpkin Rollers* by Elmer Kelton (western)
> After the Civil War, young Trey heads west to find his future. This is a western for the gents that ladies love, too.

🕮 *Seabiscuit: An American Legend* by Laura Hillenbrand (nonfiction)
> Senior audiences hoot when I confess that I didn't know who Seabiscuit was before reading this book. He was the most famous celebrity in the United States—man or beast—in 1937.

🕮 *Wait Till Next Year* by Doris Kearns Goodwin (memoir)
> A noted historian's memoir of growing up in baseball-crazed New York. Baseball fans or not, most seniors can relate to this vivid portrait of the 1950s.

Book Clubs

Is there a more perfect group in town for libraries to tie into than book discussion groups? I don't think so. Not only that, but you're likely to stumble across them in the library when they come to research their latest title or try to garner books for the group. Your task here is to tailor your information so that they realize they need your program. Market yourself as a book group resource, a special library service that they can take advantage of.

Finding Your Audience

Create a flyer with a heading such as "Attention Book Clubs" and vamp a little. If a portion of your Web site is devoted to book group recommendations, then be sure your booktalking program is mentioned, too. Your local bookstore is a great resource for you when you're dealing with book groups. They'll often have a book group registry where you can get an idea of how many book groups there are in your community and how to contact them.

I often get calls not only to speak to established book discussion groups, but also to talk to folks who'd like to start a book group but are unsure how to begin. In these instances, I preface my booktalks with a fifteen- to twenty-minute primer on the basics of book group logistics and then launch into some suggestions for great discussion books. The mechanics of choosing the books is often a stumbling block for beginning groups. When they've all heard you talk about a number of books, it makes it much easier for them to come to a decision about what to read.

Choosing Your Books

I always check our collection and make sure that there are plenty of copies of the books I talk about to book groups. But you know the circumstances of your particular library and how much support you're able to give book groups and whether this is an issue for you.

When you are choosing books for book groups, just make sure there is something in the book that can be discussed. If everyone loves it, that's great, but what is there to talk about? It might be the language or style of the book, it might be the characters and their actions, or it might be the premise and events, but it needs to be something.

Sometimes books will surprise you in their appeal for a book group. When I read *The Persian Pickle Club* by Sandra Dallas, I passed it off as a light mystery about a group of ladies in Depression-era Kansas, never thinking it had book club potential. Then a friend told me it engendered one of the best discussions her book group had ever had. The women were all keeping a secret that was revealed at the end of the book. The group had a sprightly and engaging discussion about the ethics of the situation. "How far would you go for a friend?" was the question they ended up asking each other.

Because book group members are often well read, I try to come up with titles that they might not have heard of—either brand new books or older ones that may have dropped from consciousness. Let's face it, most book clubs have read Kingsolver, Haruf, and Shreve, and it's unlikely that you have anything new to say about these authors. I was talking to the book group coordinator for a large independent bookstore the other day, and she was lamenting the fact that although they had dozens of book clubs registered with the store, they were all reading the same five titles. Make it your mission to expose book groups to the great undiscovered books that they may be missing.

I try to do a mix of heavier, profound titles with lighter titles that are discussible, but not so depressing. I generally throw in a memoir or two, because I love them and because there are so many great ones out there. I also love alerting book groups to a fabulous children's or young adult title, so I might include something like *Missing May* by Cynthia Rylant or *Mind's Eye* by Paul Fleischman. I may also include a title or two just for fun. This is a treat for you, I tell them, not necessarily a book to discuss with the group.

As I've mentioned, many book clubs never break out of choosing the "hot" literary title. See if you can broaden their horizons by booktalking some lesser-known titles. Here are some suggestions.

Lesser-Known Literary Fiction

📖 *Bee Season* by Myla Goldberg (fiction)
> Extraordinary events are unleashed when Eliza Naumann, a seemingly unremarkable nine-year-old, suddenly displays a gift for spelling.

📖 *Bel Canto* by Ann Patchett (fiction)
> A famous opera diva is hired to sing for a Japanese business titan in the home of a South American country's vice president.

📖 *Elm at the Edge of the Earth* by Robert D. Hale (fiction)
> In the idyllically rural American Midwest, between the World Wars, young David is farmed out to relatives when his mother is hospitalized with a life-threatening illness.

📖 *Ginger Tree* by Oswald Wynd (fiction)

At twenty, Scotswoman Mary MacKenzie sets sail from Scotland to China to marry her military attaché fiancé and encounters a life she hadn't expected.

📖 *Homestead* by Rosina Lippi (historical fiction)

A fictional account of the lives of women in a small Austrian village from 1909 to 1977.

📖 *In Sunlight, in a Beautiful Garden* by Kathleen Cambor (fiction)

The events and personalities, both millionaires and townsfolk, involved with the Johnstown flood.

📖 *The Jump-Off Creek* by Molly Gloss (historical fiction)

When her husband dies, Lydia Sanderson sells everything she owns and sets out to homestead in Oregon's Blue Mountains.

📖 *A Life for a Life* by Ernest Hill (fiction)

When a drug dealer holds his brother hostage, D'Ray holds up a convenience store to get the money for his release.

📖 *Lying Awake* by Mark Salzman (fiction)

Sister John of the Cross must choose between her spiritual visions and her health.

📖 *Meeting Luciano* by Anna Esaki-Smith (fiction)

Emily has just graduated from college and is staying with her mother temporarily. Her mother, Hanako, announces that's she's invited Luciano Pavarotti to the house.

📖 *Peace Like a River* by Leif Enger (fiction)

Ruben, his sister, Swede, and their father undertake an unlikely odyssey.

📖 *Year of Wonders* by Geraldine Brooks (historical fiction)

Beset by the plague in the seventeenth century, an English village quarantines itself so as not to infect neighboring towns.

Special Considerations for Book Clubs

When I'm invited to speak to book groups, I do extra homework about the group and their purpose in having me come. Is it a newly formed group still sorting out how they will choose books? Or is it a group that has been in existence for a long time and just needs some new ideas? Is it an group of older adults from a retirement home, or young moms for whom this is a respite from their duties at home? Is it a church-affiliated group? If so, do they have a particular interest in books that raise ethical or moral issues? Any book group may have a particular theme or parameters that they adhere to, and that's information that you need. We have a local multicultural book club in our service area, which makes it fun to choose books by authors of widely varying backgrounds and cultures, but that's something that's critical to know beforehand. If the group can send you a list of books they've already discussed, that's a huge help. It will give you an idea of the kind of books they choose and eliminate the possibility of you brightly and enthusiastically booktalking a list of great books that they've already read.

In talking to the coordinator of one group, I found that there was a schism between members who wanted to read "fun" books and those who wanted more literary weight. I also discovered there was a keen interest in nonfiction among some members. This information gave me lots of good clues to help me build a list that might meet their needs.

Most book group members are female. I've only seen one male at any book club meeting or event. So, given that women are more adventuresome readers than men on the whole, this is a liberating thing.

Book groups often meet in private homes and are generally smaller groups—under twenty people. This makes them an intimate audience, which sometimes translates to chatty. My booktalks become much more conversational in tone with these groups and less presentational in style. I'm much less likely to build to a cliffhanging close that works best with silence and rapt attention. These ladies have been together for a while; they are accustomed to talking to one another. They are much more likely to participate in your booktalks with opinions and comments to you and each other. It's not bad, just different, and it takes some preparation and adjustment on your part.

Community and Service Organizations

It's more than likely that your community has a Kiwanis, Rotary, or Lions Club, a chapter of the American Association of University Women, a chamber of commerce, and various business and professional women's organizations. All of them need a speaker for every meeting. Why shouldn't it be you?

Speaking to service organizations can turn into a perpetual motion machine. I spoke to one Rotary Club at the request of the director of our of library system. With very little promotion on my part, I ended up speaking to ten other Rotary Groups before the year was out. These folks talk to one another at regional conferences and cross-club visitations. Word about your presentation can get out quickly.

Finding Your Audience

The Internet and e-mail can be your best tools in contacting service organizations. Many have Web sites that list all the clubs in a region or state including officers and their contact numbers or e-mail addresses. It's a pretty simple thing to prepare a paragraph to send out via e-mail giving your program and your credentials.

Here's the kind of thing I send out, tailored to the specific organization, of course:

Take a refreshing book break . . .

Would you like to hear about great reads at the next meeting of your group or organization? Chapple Langemack, reader's services coordinator for King County Library System, is available to speak to your group on the latest and greatest, the tried and true, or just terrific books you may have missed. A veteran booktalker with an informal and humorous style, Chapple is available to do presentations from twenty to forty-five minutes long, anywhere in King County Library System. For more information, call Chapple at (123) 456-7890.

Choosing Your Books

Audience research also helps quite a lot with this group. Even these days, men will often make up the majority of a service club. So when I make up my booktalking list, I am sure to include some titles that are nonfiction, true adventure, sports related, or suspense/thrillers. I apologize if this sounds sexist, but I've found it to be true more often than not. Men and women often have different tastes in reading. The saving grace is that women are much more catholic in their tastes and will tackle anything if it sounds interesting to them. They don't care if it's a male protagonist or if it's about a sport or activity unfamiliar to them. If it sounds interesting, they'll try it. So if it's a mixed audience, but predominantly men, you can cater to male interests and still have something to offer the women.

Once a woman approached me after a Rotary meeting and asked quietly, "Do you ever see more women than this in a group?" Unfortunately, I hadn't. Her deep sigh was very telling. One Kiwanis group was the exception—nearly fifty-fifty gender distribution. My presentation was on books to give as holiday gifts, so I escaped going in with a terribly unbalanced sports/action/adventure list, but it reminded me to do my homework.

Once or twice, service club members have said they'd be interested in hearing about business-related titles. Unfortunately, in most cases I'd rather be beaten than read a business text. I won't be able to oblige, but if that's an interest of yours, here's a group that's ready for it. Books like Robert D. Putnam's *Bowling Alone*, *A Complaint Is a Gift* by Janelle Barlow, *The Tipping Point* by Malcolm Gladwell, or *Why We Buy* by Paco Underhill may be just the ticket here. And there always seems to be a recent biography of a successful CEO, be it Lee Iacocca or Jack Welch.

Here are some titles with thrills, action, and humor, both fiction and nonfiction, to consider when next you're out with the boys:

Mostly for Men

📖 *About the Author* by John Colapinto (fiction)

Cal Cunningham rockets to stardom with his first novel. There's only one problem. He didn't write it.

📖 *Cold Burial* by Clive Powell-Williams (nonfiction)

In 1926, Edgar Christian and Jack Hornby were determined to demonstrate that civilized men could survive in the Barren Grounds of the Canadian Northwest Territories. They were wrong.

📖 *The Devil's Teardrop* by Jeffery Deaver (fiction)

Retired FBI agent and documents specialist Parker Kincaid is the best hope the Bureau has of capturing the Digger, a robotlike madman on a killing spree.

📖 *Last Breath: Cautionary Tales from the Limits of Human Endurance* by Peter Stark (nonfiction)

In a fascinating blend of adventure and science, Stark recreates in heart-stopping detail what happens to our bodies and minds in the last moments of life when an extreme adventure goes awry.

📖 *The Run* by Stuart Woods (fiction)
> Senator Will Lee decides to run for president when he learns that the current vice president has Alzheimer's disease.

📖 *Voyage of a Summer Sun* by Robin Cody (nonfiction)
> Portland writer Cody takes a notion to canoe the Columbia River from source to mouth.

📖 *Windfall* by James Magnuson
> While searching for the family cat, Ben Lindberg finds eight coolers full of $500 bills in the basement of an abandoned building.

📖 *Winterdance* by Gary Paulsen (nonfiction)
> Paulsen trains to run the Iditarod.

On the other hand, if the group is all women, I let loose a little. I feel free to include rowdier titles like Jill Conner Brown's *The Sweet Potato Queens' Book of Love* or the literary equivalent of a chick flick, *Good in Bed* by Jennifer Weiner. This is especially true if it's an evening dinner program. The workday is done, food and drink has been served, and everyone's ready to kick back a little. This audience is interested in my books, yes, but they are also interested in having a good time, so I'll choose my most entertaining titles.

When it's just you and the girls, here are some fun titles to consider:

Girls Night Out

📖 *As Long as She Needs Me* by Nicholas Weinstock (fiction)
> Beleaguered Oliver Campbell is the personal assistant of the demanding Dawn of Dawn Books.

📖 *Big Stone Gap* by Adriana Trigiani (fiction)
> Pharmacist Ave Maria Mulligan fancies herself the town spinster of Big Stone Gap, Virginia, leading a mundane and unexciting life in the wake of her mother's death. Then she discovers some skeletons in the family closet, and her whole world turns upside down.

📖 *The Catsitters* by James Wolcott (fiction)

> When Johnny Downs comes home to his abandoned Manhattan apartment, he discovers that his cat sitter, who is also his girlfriend, has left more than his cat in a lurch.

📖 *Good in Bed* by Jennifer Weiner (fiction)

> Publicly humiliated in her ex-boyfriend's magazine column, Candace Shapiro decides to make a few changes.

📖 *Letters from Yellowstone* by Diane Smith (fiction)

> In the spring of 1898, promising botanist A.E. Bartram is invited to join a field study in Yellowstone National Park.

📖 *London Holiday* by Richard Peck (fiction)

> Three women find self-renewal, great shopping, and a little romance on a trip to London.

📖 *Lucy Crocker 2.0* by Caroline Preston

> Lucy, a computer-clueless mom, becomes a most unlikely cyberspace superstar.

📖 *The Perfect Elizabeth* Libby Schmais (fiction)

> As sisters Eliza and Bette grapple with men, parents, and jobs, Eliza wonders if together they wouldn't be a perfect whole.

📖 *Plain Truth* by Jodi Picoult (mystery)

> Ellie Hathaway, a big time Philadelphia defense attorney, retreats to rural Lancaster County hoping for a respite from her hectic life. Instead, she winds up defending a young Amish woman.

📖 *Space: A Memoir* by Jesse Lee Kercheval (memoir)

> Jesse Lee's family moves to Florida just as the preparation for the moonshot is in full swing.

📖 *The Sweet Potato Queens' Book of Love* by Jill Conner Brown (nonfiction)

> The Sweet Potato Queens are legendary in Jackson, Mississippi, and they'll give you all the advice you need—and then some.

Special Considerations for Service Organizations

Remember to be careful with your time constraints when you are dealing with service groups. These are often breakfast or luncheon meetings and time slots are regimented. Every Rotary Club I've dealt with has been very clear that I have only a half hour, including time for questions, and the meeting will adjourn promptly at the appointed time. Don't lose track of time and ramble on past your time slot, or you may find yourself talking to an empty room; all of your carefully choreographed points will be for naught. These are busy folk, they need to go back to work.

Note: Be wary of a situation in which a group wants you to speak while they are eating their meal. This happened to me once, due to a scheduling problem at the restaurant, and once was enough for me to vow never to do it again. The distractions are almost insurmountable: dinner is being served, and waitresses are conferring with one another on who ordered the white wine and walking in front of you to serve. There are invariably forgotten beverages or unsatisfactory orders, and all of this is going on while you are trying to maintain eye contact and command attention. All that's missing is a drunk yelling out, "Play 'Melancholy Baby'!" On top of all this, when things do calm down, your audience is looking at you and chewing. This is more unsettling than you might think. This experience gave me much empathy for stand-up comics and other nightclub performers, but this is just not a place I want to go. Speak before or after a meal, but eschew (pardon the pun) speaking during a meal.

Additional Reading

📖 Jacobsohn, Rachel W. *The Reading Group Handbook: Everything You Need to Know to Start Your Own Book Club*, revised edition. New York: Hyperion, 1998.

   This is probably the standard work on organizing and operating reading groups. There are lots of lists of suggested book group reading as well.

📖 Paz & Associates. *Reading Group Choices: Selections for Lively Book Discussions*. Nashville, Tenn.: Paz & Associates, 2000, 2001, 2002.

   Titles, summaries, brief author biographies, and sample discussion questions. Includes Web addresses for additional information when it's available.

📖 McMains, Victoria Golden. *The Readers' Choice: 200 Book Club Favorites*. New York: HarperCollins, 2000.

Tips about how to form and operate a book group are followed by a listing of books with a discussion of their appeal for book groups and a sample discussion question.

📖 Slezak, Ellen. *The Book Group Book: A Thoughtful Guide to Forming and Enjoying a Stimulating Book Discussion Group,* second edition. Chicago: Chicago Review Press. 1995.

An anthology of essays by book group members about the mechanics of a book group, with reading lists from all over the country.

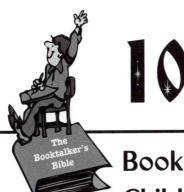

10

Booktalking to Children and Teens

Children and teenagers can be the most exhilarating and the most terrifying of booktalk audiences. Certainly adolescent scorn (or even the thought of it!) can intimidate the most confident and experienced adult. Likewise, unbridled juvenile enthusiasm can be a heady and thrilling brew.

Early on in my career, I booktalked to an eighth-grade class. Being a relative beginner, I was a little nervous but concentrated on ratcheting up the suspense on Lois Duncan's *I Know What You Did Last Summer*. Just as I was bringing the booktalk to a cliffhanger of a closing, a girl shouted out from the audience, "Can I have that book *right now*?!" It's no wonder I was hooked on booktalking forever after. Such immediate gratification is hard to resist.

I freely admit that I work especially hard on my booktalks for young people. You have less margin for error with this audience, especially teens, so I make my choices carefully and polish my hooks well. Kids, bless 'em, will immediately spot any discomfort or insincerity and will make the most of it. If you can grab them, they'll go with you anywhere, but if you lose them, it's darn difficult to get them back.

Booktalking to kids also allows you the opportunity to experiment with format and add interaction and games to your booktalks. Children are not as likely as adults to give you the hairy eyeball if you try something offbeat, and the interaction can help kids stay involved in your booktalk. Teens, on the other hand, may well give you the hairy eyeball no matter what you do, so you may as well have some fun.

Know Your Audience—Inside and Out

Before you start booktalking to children and teens, you need to make sure you have a good understanding of the developmental tasks involved in these age groups. Your group's developmental level will have an impact on their attention span, demeanor, and interests. Attention span is an obvious issue. While I might talk for forty-five or fifty minutes to a high school class, for third or fourth graders, I would only talk for twenty or thirty minutes. Those fourth graders are likely to be really vocal and responsive, whereas the teens are as likely to look like they'd rather be anyplace else. It's not necessarily disinterest, it's how their bodies and brains are linked at that developmental stage. And you may as well give up on your death glare to control teen behavior. Scientists discovered that when they showed teens photographs of faces contorted in fear or anger, they were unable to identify the emotion being expressed, while all of the adults in the study identified it correctly. So while you think you are displaying quite clearly that you are angry or annoyed, your teen audience may not have a clue. The part of the brain that is able to handle ambiguous information, make decisions, and tamp down emotion is pretty much out to lunch during the teen years.

If you don't have any background in child development, educate yourself before you head out to booktalk. It will help you know what to expect and formulate some strategies for dealing with kid behavior and for choosing books of interest. It will also help you decide how interactive you want your booktalks to be. There is some suggested reading at the end of this chapter to start you off and, later in this chapter, some ideas for games and activities to incorporate into your booktalks.

Expect the Unexpected

Every booktalk is an adventure, especially when you are booktalking to children or teens. You always need to be ready to flex and vamp and roll with the punches because things you don't anticipate will occur, no matter how well you plan. Roz still blushes when she tells this story, and she's a booktalker of many years standing:

I was booktalking at an elementary school library to three classes of hot, smelly, right-from-PE, sixth graders. I don't remember what I opened with but went into my favorite book *Rescue Josh McGuire*—a great book full of adventure, tension, and animals. The group settled down to listen to my rendition of the book . . . finished nicely. I then chose another dog story, *The Captain's Dog,* by Roland Smith. I was no sooner into my first words of the book, when I introduced the animal character named Seaman. I missed the quiet pause but definitely heard the snickers followed by the rolling laughs. After four seconds of remembering, it dawned on me that I had just introduced the dog and the group heard *semen.* My face quickly began to match my spiffy red summer reading T-shirt. The laughter just went on and on. I vaguely remembered hearing the librarian asking the group to quiet down. I was telling my face to stop getting redder. I think I said 'moving right along' and opened with some simple, plain-Jane book. I did not booktalk that title at any of the remaining schools. Even with the correct spelling of Seaman, I won't touch that title again."

Darcy also had an experience that was quite different from what she had anticipated:

 My very first booktalking experience was on September 11, 2001, of all days. The teachers were trying to keep the kids calm, and I was talking about multicultural fiction that day. There were two new girls in the class from Pakistan. I happened to be talking about a book about Pakistan, but because of the events earlier in the morning, I changed my carefully planned talk, so I would skirt the issues of Islam that I had planned to discuss. It was not that I was saying anything terrible, I just didn't want those girls to feel that they were singled out in any way."

Like I said, you need to be able to flex, vamp, and roll with the punches.

Choosing Your Books

Balance and variety are the watchwords you'll want to live by when you're choosing the books you want to booktalk to children and teens. Although it's still important for you to talk about books that you can be genuinely enthusiastic about, you need to keep in mind the particular interests of your audience. A book on snowboarding might not be on your personal hit parade, but you can appreciate the appeal of one that's well done with lots of great photos for students in that ninth-grade class that you want to lure to the library.

It's particularly important for both children and teenagers to have a variety of reading levels represented. Make sure some of your books are under the reading level for the age level you're speaking to and choose at least a couple that are more challenging. Also keep an eye out for books in which the illustrations carry the story; these can appeal to a wide age range. *The Motel of the Mysteries* by David Macaulay is one of my favorites for this purpose.

In addition to a variety of reading levels, balance your list with a variety of topics and titles. Use nonfiction as well as fiction. Booktalk some old favorites and the latest thing, the trendy and the classic. Offer sports and poetry. We so often think of teens as pack animals (wolves, not burros) who are all interested in the same thing, and it ain't necessarily so. Think of your own abiding interests as an adult. Whether it's reading, astronomy, musical theater, or baseball, you were probably exposed to it as a young person. Adolescence is when our brain is being hardwired for our skills and interests later in life, so make the most of it with your young audience. Give them a world of good things from all corners of your collection. The author Orson Scott Card once said that the best thing we can do to encourage young people to read is to offer them a banquet and let them choose.

Don't be afraid to choose some more esoteric titles as long as you have a balance. One of my library school students surprised me when he got up to do his final booktalking presentation. He began with a field guide to birds. I was dumbstruck. This seemed so adult, so removed from a teen's interest, so *borrring,* I couldn't believe he was actually booktalking this. Hadn't he listened to a thing I'd said in class all quarter? And then my canny student finished up his booktalk with, "and so, if you think you might be interested in what the boobies and the peckers in your neighborhood are doing, check out *Peterson's Field Guide to Birds.*" When I picked myself up off the floor and dried my eyes, I gave him a good grade—and not only for chutzpah. He'd shown me that you can approach just about any topic in a way that will peak a teen's interest.

Talking Fiction

Your world is almost limitless when you are choosing fiction titles to booktalk to a young audience. Ain't it grand? So think balance and variety again when you are choosing your titles. Choose some titles that seem to speak to the life of an average American kid (is there such an animal?) and some that portray a culture that may be unfamiliar. Choose a heart-rending, three-hanky story and one that has an upbeat ending.

Scary stories have a particular fascination for adolescents, possibly because risk taking is one of those adolescent developmental tasks. Horror and other frightening tales allow teens to take risks in a fictional way. Now you know why twelve-year-old boys who are reluctant to read even the skinniest book think nothing of plunging into a six-hundred-page Stephen King novel.

Active booktalkers soon find two things to be true when talking to children and teens. The first is that kids will readily read about a character older than they are but generally won't relate to a protagonist younger than they are. There are, of course, exceptions, but twelve-year-olds really seem to prefer to read about fourteen-year-olds and fourteen-year-olds are ripe for the adventures of a sixteen-year-old.

The second truism is that girls will read books about boys, but boys are not as likely to read a book with a girl as a main character. So make sure that you have titles with both male and female protagonists. As much as we tried to deny it in the sixties, gender really does make a difference. The astonishing thing is that this never changes. I recently came across a study of the reading habits of adults, which reported that women not only read much more than men, they read much more broadly. Which means that you, as a booktalker, can aim some titles directly at the boys and still have the girls come along for the ride.

For every rule there is an exception, and I don't mean to imply that kids must stay in these age and gender ghettos. As a matter of fact, I wish they wouldn't. After all, it's not the fifties anymore, thank goodness, when we believed that women exclusively stayed home (and did housework in their pearls) and men exclusively went out to work. But I do want you to be aware that this is how it falls out a lot of the time so you can be prepared for all eventualities.

Talking Nonfiction

So, holding these truths to be self-evident, it's important to have a mix in terms of gender appeal and fiction and nonfiction titles. Nonfiction titles will often appeal to reluctant readers in ways that fiction won't. There are so many interesting and wonderfully illustrated nonfiction titles out today that there's lots to choose from for your booktalks. Variety is the key here as well; include rich and tasty morsels from the less obvious parts of your collection.

Sometimes you'll be asked to key your booktalks in with a particular curriculum unit or topic. Here's how Chance handled such an assignment:

I was asked to booktalk biographies to help prepare a fourth-grade class for their research projects. The teacher asked me to bring some 'really good biographies, that the kids would really like.' So, I pulled a few items from the biographies that might interest them—sports figures, pop stars, books with lots of photographs. I also made sure to bring a few items from the reference collection, both print and Web based, that showed the students resources they might not have heard about and also resources that could help me illustrate to students how to go about doing their research."

If All Else Fails, Gross Them Out

It's a fact of life that the best way to grab and hold the attention of nine- to twelve-year-old boys (and girls) is to gross them out. I'm not suggesting you make fart noises with your armpit, although I'm sure if you wanted instruction in this technique, this is a group that would be glad to oblige. I am suggesting that you take this predilection into consideration when you are choosing your books. I like to use the story of the Franklin expedition *Buried in Ice* by Owen Beattie, which is fabulously illustrated and has lots and lots of gross-out potential, such as photos of 150-year-old shriveled corpses. Anything that will make a class say "Oooooh, gross!" in unison is prime booktalk material for this age group, and adding at least one of those titles to your list is a great idea. Here are some ideas to get you going:

Great Gross-Out Books for All Ages

For the younger set (5+)

📕 *Bug Faces* by Darlene Murawski
Look deeply into the eight eyes of the nursery-web spider and see how you fare.

📕 *It's Disgusting—And We Ate It! True Food Facts from Around the World—and Throughout History* by James Solheim
"It tastes like chicken!" Yeah, right.

📖 *My Little Sister Ate One Hare* by Bill Grossman.

> For a young audience, but a vastly entertaining counting book. It will make you think of the old woman who swallowed the fly, only grosser!

📖 *Yikes! Your Body Up Close!* by Mike Janulewicz.

> A book of microphotography of bodyscapes that look like alien planets. Yikes, indeed.

📖 *Yuck! A Big Book of Little Horrors* by Robert Sneddon

> You may never eat toast again after looking at it magnified to 35,000 times normal size.

For the older set (9+)

📖 *Animal Grossology: The Science of Creatures Gross and Disgusting* by Sylvia Branzei

> An icky concoction of real and memorable scientific facts, including how a fly eats, all about leeches, and the lowdown on bedbugs.

📖 *Body Noises*: *Where They Come from, Why They Happen* by Susan Kovacs Buxbaum and Rita Golden Gelman.

> Here's the scoop of burps, snores, sneezes, cracking bones, and gas.

📖 *Buried in Ice: The Mystery of a Lost Arctic Expedition* by Owen Beattie and John Geiger

> Forensic anthropologist Beattie found (and photographed) the bodies of sailors on the 1845 Franklin expedition, a search for the Northwest Passage that came to a tragic end.

📖 *Disgusting Digestion* by Nick Arnold

> This book answers burning questions such as, "How much pee can your bladder hold without popping?"

📖 *The Eat-A-Bug Cookbook: 33 Ways to Cook Grasshoppers, Ants, Water Bugs, Spiders, Centipedes, and Their Kin* by David George Gordon

> Recipes include Cockroach a la King and Bugs in a Rug.

📖 *Gross Grub: Wretched Recipes That Look Yucky but Taste Yummy* by Cheryl Porter
> You have to have a strong stomach to even read these recipe titles. Boogers-on-a-stick, slab o' scabs and veggie vomit, for example.

📖 *Grossology Begins at Home: The Science of Really Gross Things in Your Everyday Life* by Sylvia Branzei
> From toilets to toe jam—facts you really didn't want to know.

📖 *Man Eating Bugs: The Art and Science of Eating Insects* by Peter Menzel
> I dare you to get past the cover photo, a young woman eating deep-fried tarantula on a skewer.

📖 *Oh Yuck! The Encyclopedia of Everything Nasty* by Joy Masoff.
> From acne to maggots to vomit, it's all here.

📖 *The Rat: A Perverse Miscellany* collected by Barbara Hodgson
> A quirky compendium of rat facts, rat fiction, rat lore, and rat art.

📖 *Rats* by Paul Zindel
> When mutant rats threaten to take over Staten Island, which has become a huge landfill, fourteen-year-old Sarah and her younger brother Mike try to figure out how to stop them.

📖 *The Secret House: 24 Hours in the Strange and Unexpected World in Which We Spend Our Nights and Days* by David Bodanis
> The unsettling account of what's really happening in your house from the time you get up in the morning until you go to bed at night.

Talking Prizewinners (Even Those You Don't Like)

I talked earlier about the one time it was permissible to booktalk a book about which you're not wildly enthusiastic, and that's when you are talking to kids about nominated titles for a particular award. Most of time, this is for an award that is actually voted on by the kids based on the slate presented by the librarian. For example, the Evergreen Award is sponsored by the Washington State Young Adult Review Group, a consortium of school and public libraries that sponsor an election for kids to choose their favorites from a group of ten or twelve books chosen by librarians. This is an award based solely on popularity, not on literary quality.

If there were a clinker in the batch that I was committed to booktalking, I would find *something* about the book that I liked and could talk about. Sometimes kids' enthusiasm for a book can win you over. Maybe a particular scene or character has appeal for you. Sometimes just hearing someone else talk about the book can change how you approach it. I have often felt lukewarm about a book until I heard another librarian booktalk it. When I heard it presented in a totally different way with a fresh emphasis, I became captivated with the possibilities.

Failing that, particularly for a teen audience, I'd be perfectly honest, but in a devil's advocate sort of way. For instance, Chris Crutcher's *Whale Talk* (a book, by the way, that has great popularity with adults and teens, it just doesn't speak to me): "I really hated TJ in this book. How many kids do you know that are good enough athletes to play football, basketball, *and* be championship swimmers? Oh, then he's very smart and always has a clever, flip remark for his teachers and any other adult that annoys him. I don't know about you, but my clever remarks always come to me several hours after I needed them, so TJ really bothers me in that way." And so on. You can be perfectly free about venting your views and see if you can rope in some dissenters.

The other ploy you might use if you have some experience speaking to a class is asking if there's anyone in the class who has read the book and would like to speak to it. You can say, "This book is nominated for this award and I have really mixed feelings about it. Has anyone here read the book? Can you give me your opinion? What do you like about it?"

I offer both of these approaches as ones to be taken gently and with great caution. Rayna recalls having a similar approach go awry:

"My worst booktalking experience was in front of a sixth-grade class. I had decided to booktalk both books I liked and several I didn't like. I thought it might be interesting to compare notes with students who liked those titles, but I went about it backwards, by first asking who liked a particular book (only one sensitive young lady) and then mindlessly undercutting her by saying blandly that I found the main character to be a sort of brainless self-centered goody-goody. I think I left my common sense at home that day! Halfway through the sentence I realized what I was doing, and rushed to tag a feeble comment onto my brutal statement, saying something about how it's interesting that we look for different qualities in characters or settings etc. But I'll never forgive myself for her look of embarrassment and humiliation!"

Talking Classics

Some young adult librarians have made a specialty of booktalking the classics to teens. Talk about an instant entrée to a school! You are an English teacher's dream. "You get called in to booktalk classics when the kids have to read them, so you get better buy-in from your audience," says one young adult librarian.

It's best to talk to the teacher in some depth beforehand if you're going to do a classics booktalk. Make sure you have the same sense of which books are included in the genre and which values the classics offer that the teachers wants to reinforce.

Holly says she has a conversation with the class before she begins booktalking about just what a classic is. "I might bring a dictionary definition or an encyclopedia article. I sometimes throw out Mark Twain's quote about classics, 'A classic is something that everybody wants to have read but nobody wants to read' and see if the kids agree. I'll ask them if *Harry Potter* is a classic and why and we'll talk about themes and situations that come up in classics over and over again."

"The key to booktalking classics," says Holly, "is to engage the kids in the 'life' part of a classic, the part that resonates with all of us. Then you've got them."

Here are some examples of Holly's booktalks on titles from a spooky classics session. Holly's caveat is that these booktalks are intended for older middle school students. She says these would also work for an older audience, but she would not use them for younger students. Holly's booktalks all have such a wonderful punch at the end that I would allow a long pause for dramatic effect before I finished with the author and title.

📖 *The Invisible Man* by H.G. Wells

A man bursts into an inn in the middle of a snowstorm yelling, "A fire! In the name of human charity, a room and a fire!" He is dressed strangely: his face, head and hands are wrapped in white bandages, his felt hat is pulled down low, his eyes are shaded with strange blue glasses, and the tip of his nose is a bright, shiny pink. The innkeeper believes him to be a sick man, or a man who has suffered a horrible, disfiguring accident. The man is not sick, and he's not disfigured. Without the bandages and hat and glasses and false nose, he is invisible. He is a scientist who discovered how to make the human body invisible and tested it on himself, but cannot discover how to reverse those effects. He is quickly going insane. It's not a quiet sort of insanity—it's a violent, raging, murderous sort of insanity.

Booktalk by Holly Koelling. Reprinted with permission of the author.

📖 *Dr. Jekyll and Mr. Hyde* by Robert Louis Stevenson

Mr. Utterson is Dr. Jekyll's lawyer. He has wondered for some time why Dr. Jeykll asked him to write a will that left everything to a virtual stranger, a man named Edward Hyde. His wondering turns to concern when a relative of his relates a story to him about an incident he witnessed in which this Mr. Hyde trampled a small child on the street. The child screamed and screamed, and people came running to help her, but Mr. Hyde could not have cared less. He would have continued on his way if Mr. Utterson's relative hadn't stopped him. This relative could not, now that the event was past, remember exactly what Mr. Hyde looked like, but he did remember that there was something wrong with Hyde's appearance, he was somehow ugly and repulsive. Mr. Utterson feels its his duty as Dr. Jekyll's lawyer to investigate this Mr. Hyde and is shocked when his investigation leads him right to Dr. Jeykll's door. Dr. Jeykll is such a good and honest man, and Mr. Hyde is such a monster. What could the two have to do with each other?

Booktalk by Holly Koelling. Reprinted with permission of the author.

📖 *The Legend of Sleepy Hollow* by Washington Irving

Sleepy Hollow is a small, rural community inhabited by the descendants of Dutch settlers. The people of Sleepy Hollow are a superstitious lot and have many frightening legends about the phantoms that haunt the Hollow. The Headless Horseman is one of these legends. It is said that he's the ghost of a British soldier whose head was ripped off by a cannonball during the Revolutionary War. It's said that the ghost rides out each night from the cemetery to the battlegrounds on his black war steed in search of his missing head. Ichabod Crane is Sleepy Hollow's schoolmaster, and although he enjoys the local legends, he doesn't believe them. He's not from the area, but he would like to stay—he has his eye set on Katrina Van Tassel, the daughter of a wealthy man, and hopes he can win her hand. But so does Brom Bones, and Brom Bones is fit and handsome, while Ichabod Crane is tall and skinny and gangly. When Brom finds out that Ichabod is also interested in Katrina, the competition begins. Who's going to win, and how does the Headless Horseman come in to the action?

Booktalk by Holly Koelling. Reprinted with permission of the author.

📖 "Monkey's Paw" by W.W. Jacobs

It's a blustery night, and the Whites are cozy in their parlor. Mr. White and his son are playing chess while Mrs. White sits nearby. There's a knock on the door. It's Sergeant Major Morris, an old friend of the family, recently returned from campaigning in India. Conversation quickly goes to an object Sergeant Major Morris has brought back with him from India. It's a monkey's paw—a shriveled, mummified little paw. Sergeant Major Morris tells the Whites it had a spell put on it by a holy man, and it can grant its owner three wishes. The Whites desperately want the paw, but Sergeant Major Morris tries to warn them that having what you wish for is not always a good idea. They insist, Sergeant Major Morris reluctantly gives it to them, and what do you think they wish for first? [Get the class to talk about common wishes, one of which is usually wealth.] They get their wish. The Whites's son is horribly mutilated at the factory where he works and dies; his parents are given insurance money. If you had the monkey's paw, what would you wish for next? Mrs. White, of course, wishes for her son to come back to life. But she doesn't ask specifically for him to be put back the way he was before the mutilation. Fortunately, there's one wish left.

Booktalk by Holly Koelling. Reprinted with permission of the author.

Remember that a "classic" may also be a short story, so don't forget those while you're looking for booktalk material. When Holly booktalked the short story "The Monkeys Paw," she also demonstrated to the class how she found the story on the Internet.

Classics can also be grouped by theme. Here's a list of booktalks that Holly did for seventh-grade honors students and eighth graders, focusing on a spooky theme.

Spooky Classics

📖 *The Legend of Sleepy Hollow* (1819) by Washington Irving (1783–1859)

A superstitious schoolmaster, in love with a wealthy farmer's daughter, has a terrifying encounter with a headless horseman.

📖 *Dr. Jekyll and Mr. Hyde* (1886) by Robert Louis Stevenson (1850–1894)

A kind and well-respected doctor can turn himself into a murderous madman by taking a secret drug he's created.

📖 *The Invisible Man* (1897) by H.G. Wells (1866–1946)

The eerie story of a mad scientist who makes himself disappear and goes murderously insane when he realizes that he cannot reverse the spell.

📖 *The Old Nurse's Story* (1852) by Elizabeth Gaskell (1810–1865)

This short story warns that your own bad deeds may come back to haunt you.

📖 "The Monkey's Paw" (1902) by W.W. Jacobs (1863–1943)

This short story warns you to beware what you wish for.

Here's another list of more contemporary classics, prepared for eighth-grade honors students and ninth graders.

Modern Classics

📖 *I Know Why the Caged Bird Sings*, by Maya Angelou

This memoir traces Maya Angelou's childhood in a small rural community during the 1930s. Filled with images and recollections that point to the dignity and courage of black men and women, Angelou paints a sometimes disquieting but always affecting picture of the people and the times that touched her life.

📖 *Fahrenheit 451* by Ray Bradbury

In Ray Bradbury's classic, frightening vision of the future, firemen don't put out fires; they start them in order to burn books.

📖 *The House on Mango Street* by Sandra Cisneros

Esperanza's childhood life in a Spanish-speaking area of Chicago, on Mango Street, is described in a series of spare, poignant, and powerful vignettes.

📖 *Anne Frank: The Diary of a Young Girl* by Anne Frank

The autobiographical reminiscences of a young Jewish girl coming of age during World War II describes her life in hiding from the Nazis and offers a poignant study of the tragedy of the Holocaust.

📖 *Metamorphosis* by Franz Kafka
> A novel about a man who finds himself transformed into a huge insect and the effects of this change upon his life.

📖 *One Flew over the Cuckoo's Nest* by Ken Kesey
> An inmate of a mental institution tries to find the freedom and independence denied him in the outside world.

📖 *Flowers for Algernon* by Daniel Keyes
> Charlie Gordon, a retarded adult who cleans floors and toilets, becomes a genius through an experimental operation.

📖 *A Separate Peace* by John Knowles
> Knowles's classic story of two friends at boarding school during World War II.

📖 *To Kill a Mockingbird* by Harper Lee
> Through the young eyes of Scout and Jem Finch, Harper Lee explores with rich humor and unswerving honesty the irrationality of adult attitudes toward race and class in the Deep South of the 1930s when a black man is charged with the rape of a white girl.

📖 *Call of the Wild* by Jack London
> A bold-spirited dog is stripped from his comfortable California estate and thrust into the rugged terrain of the Klondike in this allegorical adventure story demonstrating kindness amid the bitter cold and savage lawlessness of man and beast.

📖 *The Chosen* by Chiam Potok
> The story of the friendship that develops between two Jewish boys in New York City.

📖 *Catcher in the Rye* by J. D. Salinger
> Holden Caulfield narrates the story of a couple of days in his sixteen-year-old life, just after he's been expelled from prep school.

📖 *Of Mice and Men* by John Steinbeck
> The tragic tale of a retarded man and the friend who loves and tries to protect him.

Talking Poetry

Don't forget the magical power of poetry, especially with children and teens. Poetry has a special fascination for teens. You may be surprised to know that poetry takes up the largest percentage of the nonfiction collection at the King County Youth Service Center. Not even incarcerated youth can resist poetry, it seems—especially love poetry.

Karlan, a young adult librarian, recounts this testimonial to the power of poetry:

"One of my favorite booktalk experiences occurred in the Bronx. I had taken along *Poetry in Motion,* an anthology of poems and excerpts from the project of poems placed on buses and subways, and shared a short one with the class. One young man raised his hand and asked if there were any by Dylan Thomas. There was a stanza from "Do Not Go Gentle into That Good Night," which I read. In a later class, another boy raised his hand and requested Thomas. I assumed the class was studying Dylan Thomas, but the teacher and students said, "No," and several pulled out notebooks in which they had copied that poem. They said they copied the poems they really liked when they saw them on the bus. Neither class was an honors class."

Sarah is also a great advocate of using poetry in her booktalks: "I always try to throw in a book or two of poetry and read a few of my favorite poems to promote the book. My favorite poem to booktalk is also the one that came close to getting me in trouble. It is 'The Colonel' by Carolyn Forche. It is an amazing poem, and rather disturbing and gross . . . and does mention the 'F' word. I forgot this the first time I went to read it, thinking only of the powerful effect the poem had on me when I read it to myself. Halfway through reading this to a group of eighth graders in Chicago, I realized this and had to debate what to do while reading the poem. I went with poetic integrity and said the bad word. Luckily there was a sub that day. But now when I read it, I change it slightly, telling the kids in advance that I am doing it and why, so if they want to look up the poem later they can. Clever, eh?"

Here are some tried and true collections of poetry beloved of booktalkers.

Great Poetry for Kids

For the Younger Crowd

📕 *From the Bellybutton of the Moon and Other Poems* by F.X. Alarcon
: A bilingual collection of poems in which the renowned Mexican American poet revisits and celebrates his childhood memories of summers, Mexico, and nature.

📕 *It's Raining Pigs and Noodles* (or any) by Jack Prelutsky
: Reciting "You Can't Make Me Eat That" may be just the segue you need to or from a gross book.

📕 *Kids Pick the Funniest Poems* edited by Bruce Lansky
: Try "Willie the Burper" or "Could Have Been Worse," and you'll have an entire chorus of kids joining in with you.

📕 *My Many Colored Days* by Dr. Seuss
: This rhyming story describes each day in terms of a particular color, which in turn is associated with specific emotions. One young adult librarian uses this one very successfully with middle school students.

📕 *Roald Dahl's Revolting Rhymes* by Roald Dahl
: Humorous retellings of six well-known fairy tales featuring surprise endings in place of the traditional happily-ever-after.

📕 *Sol a Sol: Bilingual Poems* written and selected by Lori M. Carlson
: A collection of poems by various Hispanic American writers that celebrate a full day of family activities.

📕 *Stopping by Woods on a Snowy Evening* by Robert Frost, illustrated by Susan Jeffers
: A beautifully illustrated rendition of this Frost poem.

📕 *Talking Like the Rain: A Read to Me Book of Poems* by X.J. Kennedy
: An illustrated collection of poems for very young children, including works by Robert Louis Stevenson, Edward Lear, Shel Silverstein, and Jack Prelutsky.

📖 *A Visit to William Blake's Inn: Poems for Innocent and Experienced Travelers* by Nancy Willard
> A collection of poems describing the curious menagerie of guests who arrive at William Blake's inn.

📖 *Where the Sidewalk Ends* (or any) by Shel Silverstein
> It's been around for a long time, but it's still a favorite. After all, who can resist a poem titled "Dancing Pants"?

For the Older Crowd

📖 *The Basket Counts* by Arnold Adoff
> Illustrations and poetic text describe the movement and feel of basketball.

📖 *Behind the Wheel* by Janet Wong
> Thirty-six poems look at various aspects of driving, including passing the written driver's test and being pulled over by a cop.

📖 *Cool Salsa: Bilingual Poems on Growing Up Latino in the United States* edited by Lori M. Carlson
> An assortment of poems that express Latino culture and the concerns of growing up in the United States.

📖 *From Both Sides Now: The Poetry of the Vietnam War* edited by Phillip Mahony
> Poetry by Americans in Vietnam as soldiers, Vietnamese children who lived through the war, and others who immigrated to the United States after the war. Best used with high school students.

📖 *Light-Gathering Poems* edited by Liz Rosenberg
> A collection of mostly classic poems that includes Dickinson, Yeats, Blake, Frost, and others.

📖 *Pierced by a Ray of the Sun: Poems About the Times We Feel Alone* selected by Ruth Gordon
> An international anthology of poems about loneliness.

📖 *The Rose That Grew from Concrete* by Tupac Shakur
> A collection of more than one hundred poems that confront topics ranging from poverty and motherhood to Van Gogh

📖 *Slam* edited by Cecily Von Ziegesar

This is teen poetry, side by side with the rants of the Beat poets, the verses of Shakespeare, and the rhymes of hip-hop. Also included is an explanation of poetry slams and writing tips for budding poets.

📖 *Stone Bench in an Empty Park: Haiku* edited by Paul Janeczko
An anthology of haiku accompanied by photographs reflects nature in the city.

📖 *Stop Pretending: What Happened When My Big Sister Went Crazy* by Sonya Sones
A younger sister has a difficult time adjusting to life after her older sister has a mental breakdown.

📖 *A Suitcase Full of Seaweed and Other Poems* by Janet Wong
Wong reflects on her Korean and Chinese heritage in these poems.

📖 *Teen.com Book of Poetry* edited by Missy Rekos
Poems of love, family, friendship, and life written by teens from around the world.

📖 *Things I Have to Tell You: Poems and Writing by Teenage Girls* edited by Betsy Franco
Poems, stories, and essays written by girls aged twelve to eighteen that speak about body image, seduction and betrayal, courage and failure, shame and pride.

📖 *Who Killed Mr. Chippendale?* by Mel Glenn
Free verse poems describe the reactions of students, colleagues, and others when a high school teacher is shot to death as the school day begins.

📖 *You Hear Me? Poems and Writing by Teenage Boys* edited by Betsy Franco
An anthology of stories, poems, and essays by adolescent boys on love, anger, sex, "monster" drugs, family, conformity, and being gay.

In addition to using poetry in her booktalks, Jeani likes to give students an opportunity to share a favorite poem or poetry they have written themselves. In the following anecdote, Jeani describes one of her booktalking excursions:

Every class had at least one shy student who eventually found the courage to choose to read a poem out loud. Another neat thing was that every class had at least one student who could read Spanish, so they were able to read a few of the bilingual poetry books. Finally, one of the classes had a student read aloud her own original poetry that was really good. It was a special day. Sharing poetry is really a fun, easy, and compelling way to booktalk to a class."

You can include poetry in with your other booktalks, or you can do an exclusively poetical program. Here's a sample of what Jeani did for an all poetry program at a middle school:

An All-Poetry Booktalk

Poems Shared

- 📖 "Almost Ready" from *Slow Dance Heart Break Blues* by Arnold Adoff
- 📖 Three poems from *A Joyful Noise: Poems for Two Voices* by Paul Fleischman: "Book Lice" [listen to tape], "Water Striders" [kids read to classmates], "Honeybees" [kids read to classmates]
- 📖 "Harlem" from *Earth-Shattering Poems* edited by Liz Rosenberg
- 📖 "I Look at You" from *When the Rain Sings: Poems by Young Native Americans*
- 📖 Two poems from *Night Garden: Poems from the World of Dreams* by Janet Wong: "Old Friend" and "Nightmare"

Booktalks

📖 *Foreign Exchange: A Mystery in Poems* by Mel Glenn

📖 *Make Lemonade* by Virginia Euwer Wolff

📖 *Out of the Dust* by Karen Hesse

Talking Graphic Novels

Graphic novels may look like comic books, but their content can be deadly serious. Whatever the topic, the format has lots of appeal to many teens, so you may want to include them in your booktalks. If you are booktalking in a school setting, Kirsten warns, know that "some teachers view them similarly to videos or magazines—i.e., 'junk reading' (grrr)."

If you'd like to give them a whirl, here are some titles to try recommended by young adult librarian and graphic novel aficionado Dawn Rutherford.

Graphic Novels

📖 *Bone* (series) by Jeff Smith
Excellent for all ages, good adventure/fantasy tale. I've heard very good feedback from teachers and parents whose teen "nonreaders" have eaten up this series.

📖 *Little Lit: Folklore & Fairy Tale Funnies* edited by Art Speigleman
Good for younger teens. I always tell them this is too weird and creepy for little kids, so don't show this to your brothers or sisters.

📖 *Maus* and *Maus II* by Art Speigleman
Because it gets the idea into teachers' heads that graphic novels can be literature. History! Pulitzer Prize! Holocaust survival!

📖 *Pedro and Me: Friendship, Loss and What I Learned* by Judd Winick
True story about someone who was on MTV . . . what more do you need?

⬛ *The Tale of One Bad Rat* by Bryan Talbot

> Best for high school–age kids. Tale of an abused girl obsessed with Beatrix Potter, who goes on a journey across England to confront her personal demons.

So I'll say it again, variety and balance is the key. Be bold, try out lots of different titles. Experiment. But remember that every class dynamic is different, and what dies with one class may be a smash hit with another, so give any book a couple of auditions before you ban it from your repertoire forever.

Props, Costumes, and Games

Many youth services librarians like to use some participatory techniques as an attention getter. These kinds of activities help involve kids who are just not ready to sit and listen for a prolonged period of time. You might want to spread out all the books and have the children choose which book they want to hear about next. Or here's a good spot for props. You can have a prop for each book and have the children choose the booktalk by choosing the item. One children's librarian takes a suitcase full of props that match up to the books she's brought. Then she asks a child to reach in and choose something. They don't get to peek! Then she launches into the booktalk that pairs up to the chosen prop.

Peg, a young adult librarian, counts the following booktalking session as one of her best ever.

A colleague told me about a booktalking technique that had worked well for her. She said she had procured an object for each book she was going to booktalk. A teen from the audience chose an item and that determined which book she would booktalk. She proceeded to demonstrate that technique by using an apple to stand in for the book *In My Hands: Memories of a Holocaust Rescuer* by Irene Gut Opdyke. I started collecting items immediately for the books I was reading and was ready to rock and roll for the next Teen Read Week's booktalks. I found that it really grabbed the teens' interest and kept them involved. They really got into the spirit of things; even coming up to the table to make their choices. This led into some spontaneous interplay between the kids and myself. If they chose the Monopoly money, I could ask them if they were rich. When they would say, "No, the money was counter-feit," and that would lead right into my introduction for the book, *Counterfeit Son* by Elaine Marie Alphin. Using this technique led to serendipitous things happening, like the cool, tall eighth-grade boy named Eduardo, who came up and chose the watering can for *Esperanza Rising* by Pam Munoz Ryan. But care needs to be used in choosing appropriate props. Even though I was never challenged about my use of a toy gun, pur-chased at the Dollar Store, I could have used something else to sell *Give a Boy a Gun* by Todd Strasser. After all, I used a CD of the Supremes singing "Stop in the Name of Love" to sym-bolize Sonya Sones's book *Stop Pretending*."

Elizabeth Panni, a seasoned children's librarian at a public library, has got this prop thing handled. Here are some of her tips.

The Queen of Props Speaks

I am a great yard sale/thrift store shopper. I am always on the lookout for props. Sometimes the prop shows up, and I can imme-diately think of a book to match it to; other times I search for a prop that will work with a book I want to booktalk. For example, one day I happened across a saltshaker that was in the shape of an overstuffed chair. The first thing I thought of was the book *A Chair for My Mother*. It went into the prop box.

Here are some other ideas I've used for props:

- A large pebble for *Sylvester and the Magic Pebble* by William Steig
- Paper dolls for *The Five Sisters* by Margaret Mahy
- A pen for *Frindle* by Andrew Clements
- Antlers for *The Great Antler Auction* by Susan Goodman
- Mukluks for *The Year of Miss Agnes* by Kirkpatrick Hill
- An empty grape juice bottle or perfume bottle for *Attaboy, Sam!* by Lois Lowry
- A small button for *The Bone Detectives* by Donna M. Jackson
- A baseball for *Patrick Doyle Is Full of Blarney* by Jennifer Armstrong
- A baseball card for *Honus and Me* by Dan Gutman

- A plastic bat (the critter) for *Zipping, Zapping, Zooming Bats* by Ann Earle
- A large decorated paper Z for *The Story of Z* by Jeanne Modesett
- A small milk carton for *The Face on the Milk Carton* by Caroline Cooney

When I booktalked Mary Downing Hahn's book *A Time for Andrew: A Ghost Story,* I bought some marbles, scrounged up a little drawstring bag, and attached a small note to the drawstring that said, "WARNING! These marbles belong to Andrew Joseph Tyler. If you take them you will be sorry. 7 June 1910." It was complete with skull and crossbones on the note, just as the book describes. I had one little boy ask me if they were the *real* marbles that the boy in the story had found.

Rayna used a costume and a game to good effect. Here's what she says:

My fondest booktalking memory was the spring we were using mystery as a theme for our summer reading program. I think I had an especially good experience in classes because of two things: one was that I dressed up as Sherlock Holmes and carried a briefcase full of candy with me. The other was that I made a list of mystery fiction with an attached quiz. I placed the illustrated covers of the books facing out on a table or bulletin board in the front of the class, and the annotations on the list of titles also gave clues. I asked each class to take a few minutes at the beginning to answer the questions, and then we went through them (several were odd or amusing), and I tagged short booktalks onto the answers. Then I reward them by allowing each person to take a piece of candy as I walked through the room talking about the summer reading program and the special events we had planned."

Some children's librarians use games based on *Wheel of Fortune* or *Jeopardy* for upper-elementary students. The children spin a dial or roll a cube to determine which booktalk comes next. One librarian uses a *Jeopardy* format and has the student answer in the form of a question, just like the real game. One *Jeopardy* answer might be, "The name of a well-known dog sled race in Alaska." The response is, "What is the Iditarod?" which leads into a booktalk of *Woodsong* by Gary Paulsen. Another answer might be, "The first woman to fly across the Atlantic alone," prompting the question, "Who was Amelia Earhart?" and a booktalk for *Living Dangerously: Women Who Risked Their Lives for Adventure*. If you choose to use this technique, make sure you vary the difficulty of the questions.

Using Music and Recordings

Here's what one young adult librarian from a public library has to say about using recordings in her booktalks:

> I almost always bring in cassettes in which I'll play an excerpt from a book on tape version of a book or a skit from Garrison Keillor or a poetry reading. This is just to break up the monotony of the focus being on me the whole time, plus it gives me a break. Some of my cassette recordings are really 'tried and true' since they are always well-received."

Another young adult librarian has used music successfully in her booktalks:

> One of my most memorable experiences was booktalking Joyce McDonald's *Swallowing Stones,* and right before it I played a song by Cheryl Wheeler called "If It Were Up to Me." The teens were mesmerized by the song, and it set the mood for listening to that particular booktalk. I usually booktalk a number of books at once, and I saved this one for last. It was very quiet in the room. It usually is when I booktalk, but this was a different kind of quiet . . . a stillness of them thinking."

Closing Thoughts

When you booktalk to children and teens, don't fear the opportunity to take kids to a newer, even a higher ground. Don't condescend or patronize. Don't admonish their favorite pastimes or silly (to you) obsessions. Speak clearly, with confidence, and with a sense of humor. Be yourself. If you have chosen and prepared well, the books should speak for themselves—just don't get in their way. Allow the books the time and space to fill the room when you speak of them, not necessarily with reverence, but more with a sense of wonder and mystery and joy.

Additional Reading

On Child Development

📖 Bradley, Michael J. , Ed. D. *Yes, Your Teen Is Crazy: Loving Your Kid Without Losing Your Mind.* Gig Harbor, Wash.: Harbor Press, 2002.
    Includes very readable chapters on the adolescent brain and adolescent insanity.

📖 Brownlee, Shannon. "Inside the Teen Brain" *U.S. News & World Report* (August 9, 1999), p. 44.
    The latest on teen brain research.

📖 Gopnik, Alison, Andrew N. Meltzoff, and Patricia K. Kuhl. *The Scientist in the Crib: What Early Learning Tells Us About the Mind.* New York: Harper Trade, 2000.
    Good information on child development issues.

On Booktalking to Children and Teens

📖 Bromann, Jennifer. *Booktalking That Works.* New York: Neal-Schuman, 2001.
    Features research about teen reading interests plus information of booktalking methods and sample booktalks.

📖 Jones, Patrick. *Connecting Young Adults and Libraries: A How to Do It Manual,* second edition. New York: Neal-Schuman, 1998.
    Patrick clearly lays out the mechanics of booktalking in the chapter "Booktalking: Don't Tell, Sell."

📖 Schall, Lucy. *Booktalks Plus: Motivating Teens to Read.* Englewood, Colo.: Libraries Unlimited, 2001.
    Booktalks grouped in topics relating to curriculum and to adolescent developmental tasks. Includes a summary of the book and related activities.

On Choosing Your Books

📖 Baxter. Kathleen A., and Marcia Agness Kochell. *Gotcha! Nonfiction Booktalks to Get Kids Excited About Reading.* Englewood, Colo.: Libraries Unlimited, 1999.

    Lots of suggestions here for topics and specific nonfiction titles to use with elementary and middle school students. Also look for Baxter's column on nonfiction booktalks in *School Library Journal.*

📖 Baxter, Kathleen A., and Marcia Agness Kochell. *Gotcha Again!* Englewood, Colo.: Libraries Unlimited, 2002.

    Even more suggestions of nonfiction titles to use with students.

📖 Carter, Betty. *Best Books for Young Adults: The History, the Selections, the Romance.* Chicago: American Library Association, 1994.

    Good information of the history of American Library Association's Best Books for Young Adults, plus a gold mine of potential booktalking titles for teens from BBYA lists through the years.

📖 Odean, Kathleen. *Great Books About Things Kids Love: More Than 750 Recommended Books for Children 3 to 14.* New York: Ballantine, 2001.

    Good browsing for nonfiction booktalk titles from baseball to cowboys to poetry plus lots and lots of critters.

📖 Rochman, Hazel. *Tales of Love and Terror: Booktalking the Classics, Old and New.* Chicago: American Library Association, 1987.

    Good advice on building your booktalks. Particularly helpful on figuring out how to approach your book and how to choose passages to read aloud.

📖 Rothschild, D. Aviva. *Graphic Novels: A Bibliographic Guide to Book-Length Comics.* Englewood, Colo.: Libraries Unlimited, 1995.

    Includes an in-depth explanation of what graphics novels are and an annotated bibliography of graphic novels by genre.

📖 Weiner, Stephen. "Beyond Superheroes: Comics Get Serious." *Library Journal* (February 1, 2002), p. 55.
   A good, brief introduction to graphic novels.

Web Sites and Listservs

- The American Library Association's Young Adult Library Services Association gathers together many useful booktalking tools and ideas, plus a great list of resources on adolescent development at http://www.ala.org/yalsa/profdev/

- You can join a booktalking discussion group at http://groups. yahoo. com/group/booktalking

Booktalking in Schools

If you are a public librarian serving youth, then you will most often find your audience in a school setting. Making your contacts and arrangements can be challenging but ultimately very satisfying when you see those kids back in your library. Says Sharon, a children's librarian from a public library, "The best thing about booktalking for me is the kids getting excited and talking about books they have read and then coming into the library to talk more about books and check out my booktalk selections. This happens every time, and I love working with these fabulous people."

Getting In

Schools can be the promised land of booktalking for a youth services librarian. After all, there's your audience right there waiting for you. Getting into schools can also be like infiltrating Fort Knox. Teachers have their hands full with a mandated curriculum to try and get through during the year and may not welcome outside interruptions. This means it's up to you not only to let them know about your services, but to show how your booktalks tie into their educational plan. You also need to make sure they understand that what you do is support for them, not more work on their plate.

The place to start is with homework—for you. Find out the name of the principal and school librarian. If it's a high school, check for the head of the English or language arts department. The school's Web site is a terrific way to search for this information. See if they are using a whole language approach, one that emphasizes reading from complete sources rather than

129

excerpted chapters. Prepare a concise spiel on benefits that booktalking provides: it motivates the students to read, exposes them to titles that they might not otherwise be aware of, and ties into the curriculum in ways you've discovered in your homework. Now you're ready to start making contacts.

If you have a child who attends school in the district you'd like access to, perhaps your child's teacher is the place to start gathering information. Talk to the teacher, explain what you'd like to do, and ask for advice on how to proceed and for names of others in the school district whom you might contact.

Generally, it's accepted protocol for public librarians to start by contacting the school librarian. It's a collegial courtesy. You may already know each other from book review meetings; if so that's great. Make an appointment to chat for ten minutes, either on the phone or in person, about what it is you're offering. Leave something tangible for the librarian to give to teachers. Ask about other people in the building you should contact. The school librarian may be willing to arrange for you to booktalk to classes in the library.

One savvy public librarian would leave a stack of business cards with the school librarian who kept them on her desk. Every time a teacher came in with the question, "Who was that public librarian?" the school librarian was able to whip a card off her desk and present it to the teacher. Mission accomplished.

Your next step is contacting the school principal. Call or e-mail and make an appointment. I think it's important for the principal to see your face. If you are asking for entrance into his or her school, the principal needs to scope you out. Go explain the program and the benefits to the students. Leave contact information. Ask for ten minutes at a faculty meeting to talk about the program. Failing that, ask for permission to have a letter or notice put in every teacher's mailbox. Ask if there are any teachers who might be particularly interested. Send a thank you note after your conversation. The principal's time is a big gift, make sure you show you appreciate it.

A word here about contacting school folk. E-mail is a terrific for this; don't hesitate to use it. Public librarians often work nights and weekends; school librarians usually do not. Trying to find a time for each of you to be at the other end of a phone is problematic in the extreme. Teachers are even harder to get in touch with. If there isn't a phone in the classroom, they have to be called out of class to answer. If there is a phone in the classroom, your call may be an unwelcome interruption. E-mail on the other hand can be read and answered at a convenient moment and forwarded to whomever else the recipient thinks is interested. Just think, if you e-mail the principal a brief message on your availability to booktalk, he or she can forward it to the rest of the faculty with one stroke.

Talking to the Faculty

Getting time at a school faculty meeting is the Holy Grail for a public librarian. If you are ceded this bonanza, prepare well and use your time wisely. Be quick, polished, and entertaining. Be confident and positive about what you have to offer. Make sure that the teachers leave your presentation with information that is truly useful to them. Don't just explain your booktalking program, give them a brief sample. Tell them what other services you can offer, whether it's helping to develop a new booklist or gathering titles for a specific assignment. And take a few minutes at the end to give them something just for them. Talk about a new book that's come in that would be useful for teachers or just plain fun. Talk about something like *Educating Esme* by Esme Raji Cordell, a great, funny book about a teacher's first year.

Try to arrange to be first on the agenda at the faculty meeting. JoAnn, a former school librarian who knows her onions about such things, makes the following observation: "If the faculty meets before school, the teachers will be increasingly anxious to go and get ready for class as the meeting progresses. If the meeting is held after school, the faculty will be increasing anxious to get out and go home as the meeting goes on." Either way you are much better served being first on the agenda. Once you've completed your presentation, leave the meeting. You don't want to sit through the faculty's other business, and they don't necessarily want you there listening to every word.

Once you've gained entrée into a school, throw your cap in the air and celebrate. That is a great achievement. Continue to work with the school to develop an ongoing plan of when to offer your booktalks. If you can key in to particular units or events on a regular basis, then your booktalks become a part of the rhythm of the school year. And that's a good thing. Many children's librarians try to make their visits to elementary schools in the fall, to tie in with library card promotions, and in the late spring, to tie in with the public library's summer reading program. Young adult librarians may find it easier to piggyback with a particular unit of study in the English or social studies or history department. Some schools ask that students do "reading wheels"—that is, read one book in a number of different genres. Some schools integrate English and social studies and require students to read a book set in a particular place or during a particular time period. Your booktalks might be just the kickoff for these kinds of programs. Investigate and look for opportunities to tie into on a regular basis.

Personal Relationships Are Key

JoAnn VanderKooi, a school librarian who now works for a large public library system, has particularly good insight and ideas when it comes to communicating with school folk:

> Nancy, the public librarian who served my school, was one smart cookie. She used to stop in every couple of months, just briefly. She knew when school ended and when I left for the day, so she chose a time just after school when she knew I wouldn't be distracted with other duties. She would always bring me something of interest from the public library and stayed to chat for five or ten minutes. After several visits I felt very comfortable with her, and we developed a great working relationship.
>
> Now that I work for the public library as the liaison to schools, I find that a personal relationship is critical. When I call or e-mail school staff that I have been able to meet face to face, I get an immediate response. When I try to contact school officials that I have yet to meet, the response is not as good. Sometimes I get no response at all. Building a good relationship is definitely the key to working with schools."

Rules for Schools

If you are a school librarian you know the protocol and institutional culture, but public librarians may not be as aware. When you are booktalking in schools there are some things you need to take into consideration. So listen up here to Auntie Chapple's advice.

Never Booktalk Alone

Rule number one for a public librarian booktalking in a school setting is that you are never on your own. Even if there are two of you booktalking as a team, the teacher or school librarian should always be present. There are several reasons for this. The most obvious one has to do with discipline issues. Your group may be angels with perfect deportment, or they may be the Class from Hell. Whichever the case, your job is to booktalk, not to make sure Max isn't committing mayhem. This should be something you cover in your initial contact. Be very clear that the teacher or school librarian must remain in the room. This is not negotiable. "Just tell them that you are a public librarian," is Holly's advice, "Remind them that you have no training in class management and that the teacher or the school librarian needs to be there."

Some of us learned this lesson the hard way. Many years ago I went into a high school classroom to give a presentation. It wasn't booktalking this time, I was giving research tips for the big paper everyone had pending. The teacher left the room and immediate pandemonium ensued. The students were interested neither in me nor the information I had to offer, no matter how useful it was or entertaining I was. After a few futile minutes, I announced to the class, without rancor, that it was clear this wasn't the day for this material and I left. I stopped by the office on my way out to let them know there was an unattended class and went back to my library.

Another reason that you should never be alone with a group to booktalk in a school setting is a sad commentary on our litigious society. There needs to be another adult in the room lest there be an issue of inflammatory or improper behavior. It's a fact of life that by the time a comment or action is filtered through a child to a parent and back to a school official, it may have changed from perfectly innocent to wildly offensive. You need another set of eyes and ears in the room for insurance.

Be Respectful of Your Audience and of Yourself

When you're talking to children and teens, whatever the setting, you need to bring the same honest enthusiasm for the books that you would to any audience. Take care not to pander or talk down to a younger audience. "I never presume that kids will like the book," says Elizabeth, "I just share my own reactions and responses and suggest it as one to consider."

Dealing with a group of kids can sometimes be intimidating, especially for the novice. If you run into a response that's uncomfortable or hurtful, ignore what you can and respond honestly when possible. When a student said something unkind to Holly during a booktalk, she responded this way: "Hey! You really hurt my feelings. Why did you say that?" She got an immediate and contrite apology from the student involved. Remember that you are a visitor, and not the disciplinarian. It's not up to you to make the students behave. Make sure you don't threaten or cajole. One young adult librarian says her favorite line to an obstreperous class is, "If you don't calm down, I don't think I can talk, and I was really looking forward to talking to you." Of course, she is perfectly sincere, and it generally works like a charm. If the situation is too out of control, then leave. You have no obligation to stay in such a circumstance.

Jeani had a learning experience with a booktalk that she was not too happy about at the time:

> ❝❝ The teacher sitting in the back of the room was completely oblivious to the students' nearly complete disrespect for me. They were talking while I was talking, walking around while I was talking, and who knows what else. I learned after this episode to insist on a teacher's active involvement and attention to discipline while I was in the class—or to exercise my option to leave."

The moral to this story is not that teenagers or children are unruly beasts, but that you must have respect for yourself as well as for them. There is absolutely no reason to suffer this kind of reception. If the situation is out of hand, then politely excuse yourself and leave. It's not your job to outshout anyone and if that's what it's down to, then it's unlikely anyone will benefit. Call it a day and try again later.

Be Mindful of the Books You Choose

School libraries and public libraries have of necessity different stances when it comes to intellectual freedom. Public libraries can and do have something to offend everyone. Their role is to make a vast array of literature and information available to a large and varied public. Public librarians assume that it's up to individuals to choose for themselves and their children that which meets their needs. Public libraries do not act as parental substitutes but instead try to give parents the information they need to guide their own child's reading. Using the public library is a totally optional endeavor.

School, on the other hand, is a mandatory activity, and the institution does act *in loco parentis.* School libraries are charged with supporting the curriculum and must be more circumspect in choosing recreational reading for students. Parents are very sensitive to, and vocal about, the books that can be found in the school library. So when you as a public librarian bring books in to booktalk in a school you need to be mindful of the different standards. Books that have explicit sex scenes or foul language are not going to be warmly received. Violence, too, is an increasingly touchy issue. (The irony here, of course, is that those books adults find the most distasteful are often just the books teens in particular are most eager to read.)

I've heard public librarians get on their intellectual freedom high horse and declare they'll take whatever books they choose to a school, no matter how controversial the book may be. In theory, this is your right. In practice, you will make the host institution extremely uncomfortable and open the school staff up to parental complaints. Under these circumstances, what do you think is the likelihood of you being invited back? It would be better by far to use some sensitivity in the books you select to booktalk, develop a great relationship with the school folk, and get those kids into the public library where they can choose from the full range of what you have to offer.

Schools will rarely ask to see a list of what you talk about beforehand (although I have heard of some parochial schools that do). They depend on your good judgment as a professional and your respect for the standards of the institution involved.

Make the Books Available

When you are booktalking to children and to teens it's especially important to have the books readily available to them. It's heartbreaking to build up that rush of enthusiasm only to disappoint by not having enough books. If you are a public librarian and it works for you to bring the books into the school situation to check out, that's fine. If the point is to entice the students into the public library to get the books, that's great, too. Just be sure you've chosen paperbacks or other books of which you can have multiple copies. Also make sure you've given the students, as well as the school librarian and your own library staff, a list of the books you've talked (remember the Golden Rule!). Make sure everyone on your library staff knows where in the library you post a list of the books that you booktalked in the school and where that stash of actual books is kept so everyone can point the clamoring throngs in the right direction.

Clever Colleen, a young adult specialist in a public library, had a low-tech method for getting books to kids. After she booktalked in a classroom, she passed around a tablet of paper. Each student could write down his or her library card number and the titles of the books he or she wanted to request. When Colleen returned to the library, she entered the holds for each student.

Bruce, on the other hand, was able to engineer a high-tech method. He found out how to dial in to his library's circulation system from the middle school where he was booktalking. Having done that, it was easy to check out the students' books, just as if they were at the public library. This had the added advantage of not putting him in the position of discovering major fines or lost items that block a student's card after he trudged back to the library with a handwritten list. This technique is particularly effective if you are able to bring multiple copies of each title with you.

If you decide to check out books to students on site at the school but don't have a lot of copies of each title, then you'll need to give some thought to how you'll decide which students get which books. One school librarian sheepishly confessed that after she finished booktalking, the students ran across the full length of the library to snatch up the books. While that's certainly gratifying and a fabulous testament to her booktalking skills, she admitted it wasn't the best way to distribute the books. Maybe you'd want to consider something as simple as putting each student's name in a hat. The first name pulled gets his or her choice of books, the second gets to choose from the remainder and so on.

Here's one more small thought when you are choosing your books to take to a school. The public library may often have new books sooner than the school library, or that's what my school librarian friends tell me. So be sure you have some older titles in your booktalking bag so the school librarian can back you up with her collection. She wants to play, too. As a matter of fact, you might want to check with the school librarian a week or two before your booktalk to coordinate titles and give her an opportunity to pull your booktalk titles and readalikes she might have in her collection in advance.

Closing Thoughts

It may take some effort for public librarians to find their booktalking audience in schools, but if kids are what you after, it's the perfect place to go. If you're respectful of the time, mission, and institutional culture of the folks involved, and if you're able to market yourself as an important addition to the educational process, you're set up for success in school booktalking. You, too, may get words of praise like these from your school superintendent: "The support of the library has contributed significantly to the fact that our school district achieved its reading goal. It takes all of us working together, and we could not ask for a better partner in this all-important endeavor."

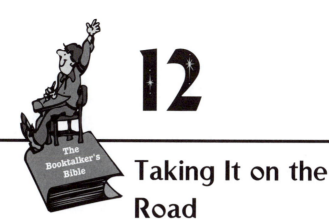

12

Taking It on the Road

You've researched, you've prepared, you've rehearsed, and you're ready to go. Let's walk through a day of booktalking and see how it goes, sort of a mental checklist before you actually go out in the world.

What Shall I Wear?

There may be some folk in the world who wouldn't fret over this issue, but I have yet to meet them. You're going to be talking in front of a group of people, for heaven's sake, it's natural to give a thought to your appearance. The most important thing about your clothes is being able to forget about them. Fidgeting with ill-fitting clothing or shoes that don't feel right isn't going to cut it. You want to focus all your energies on your presentation. You want to be able to move freely. You're going to be on your feet for a while, especially if you are doing several classes in a school, so comfy tootsies are important. In general, less is probably more in terms of stylish furbelows. You want people focused on your face, not a clever detail on your jacket. Aim for clean, comfortable, and professional.

I dress somewhat differently depending on my audience. If I'm addressing the Rotary, the Chamber of Commerce, or any other group of high-rolling business types, I wear a suit, maybe not pinstripes, but definitely a suit. It levels the playing field and lets me begin at their level. For other audiences, I wear my normal work attire—slacks or skirt and a nice blouse with a vest, sweater, or jacket—casual business attire. I think a suit overpowers a community group or book club. You want to look approachable but still come across as someone who knows what they're talking about.

Our library system often underwrites T-shirts to promote our summer reading program, and many youth services librarians wear those in their spring visits to schools or dress in a way relating to the theme of the summer. Again, be comfortable with what you choose. If you have fun dressing up and don't feel self-conscious, then go for it.

I know that some young adult librarians wear jeans to booktalk in schools, and I guess I'd be showing my age to admit it makes me a little twitchy. Are jeans what you'd normally wear to work? Are they what the teachers in the school wear? I think wearing your normal work clothes shows respect to your audience, and it's more important to respect your audience than to try to *be* your audience. So now I guess I'm a card-carrying old curmudgeon. Who'd have thought it?

Okay, you're dressed and ready. Let's move on. On the following page, you'll find a list of things you'll need to take with you.

Packing Your Bags

Let's think through what you're going to take with you:

- ☐ First of all, the books or book dummies depending on which you prefer.

- ☐ Multiple copies of the list of books you'll be talking about. Remember to include your name and contact information on it.

- ☐ Any other handouts or booklists you'll need.

- ☐ Your driving directions and map or road atlas.

- ☐ Evaluation forms.

- ☐ Whatever equipment you need if you are going to do any kind of ersatz checkout.

- ☐ Paper and pencil—there'll likely be someone who wants information from you or who wants to tell you about a great book they've just read.

- ☐ Are you going to issue library cards on site? Then you better take the applications and the cards.

- ☐ A stack of business cards.

- ☐ A water bottle.

- ☐ Tissues. I know I sound like your mother now, but I have been at booktalks where my nose inexplicably starting running, and I had no tissues with me, nor were there any in the room. I spent the whole booktalk sniffing—an ugly thing to listen to— and resisting the impulse to wipe my nose on my sleeve.

- ☐ Makeup. If you wear it, take it. Debbie tells the story of being dressed and groomed to the nines for a job interview and having a bug fly in her eye in the car on the way. After twenty minutes of tearing and swearing, she had half of a perfectly made up face and nothing with her with which to repair the damage.

- ☐ A sweater or jacket—you never know if your room will be boiling or freezing.

- ☐ Lunch or a snack. This is particularly important if you are going to be there for several hours. Performing, which is what you're doing, takes a lot out of you. Keep your energy up.

I cannot resist reading "how to pack" manuals and, as a result, have become addicted to Ziploc or other sealable plastic bags. Plus, it rains a lot in Seattle, and it's a great way to keep things dry. I use the largest size Ziploc and put a tablet and a couple of pens in it plus my business cards. In another bag, I put the handouts for the day. Why two bags? Well, I'm an anal retentive Virgo and a librarian besides. I can't help it. The other reason is that the contents of one bag remains constant, refilled after each booktalk; the other changes each time. Besides, two large bags just cover the top of my book bag so that my books are protected.

Speaking of book bags . . . I mostly do one-shot booktalks these days and find that a large book bag is just about right for the number of books I need for a thirty- to forty-five-minute presentation; two bags will do for an hour. However, if you're doing several booktalks, possibly to varied audiences, that requires more materials. A book bag probably won't work as well for you. Look through an office supply catalog and see what's available. I use those collapsible plastic crates when I have tons of stuff, although they can get heavy when filled to the brim. I've tried the crates in conjunction with a fold-up luggage carrier, which should work well, but seems to be beyond my mechanical capabilities. There weren't enough bungee cords in the world to keep that crate from sliding off that luggage dolly. Plus I still had to hoist the crate full of books in and out of the car. They do make crates now that have their own wheels, kind of a little red wagon approach. That may be worth a try. It will take a few times for you to get the feeling for what you really need and the best way to tote it.

Getting There

Think about how early you need to be at your destination. When did you tell the contact person you'd arrive? How much time do you need in addition to transit time? Is it a large complex? Will you need to offload your books and supplies and then park farther away? Will it take you additional time to find the particular building you need among many on the campus? Are you going to a meeting where the sound system is already set up, or will you need time to set up and test it? Will the chairs be set up in advance (I hope!)? How much time will it take you to set up your display of books? How is traffic at that time of day in that area? Is weather likely to be an issue? If one snowflake falls in Seattle, the whole region flies into a panic, so weather is definitely an issue in winter here. Is there a ferry schedule to be considered? (Sorry, I had to throw that one in. We do have an island in our service area that is served only by ferry.)

So figure out how much time you'll need in addition to travel time. Then, if you're going to an unfamiliar place, add ten minutes of lost time. I have absolutely no sense of direction, so if I get lost, it's generally a doozie. The driving directions on Mapquest and other Web utilities have helped a lot and most of the time I do pretty well, but there are certain areas of the county that just buffalo me, no matter how many times I visit. So I just add some extra "lost time" for those areas, which pretty much ensures that I drive right to my destination. I use the extra time to warm up, relax in the car for a few minutes, or review my books.

Checking In and Setting Up

When I get to my destination I generally leave the books in the car to start, especially if there's a lot of them. I go inside and find the restroom. (I did tell you this was a nitty-gritty sort of a guide, didn't I?) This is the time to comb your hair, check your makeup, see if there's spinach between your teeth, check your hem or your fly, or do whatever sort of ablutions calm and center you and make you feel ready to roll. Take care of anything you don't want to intrude on your consciousness for the next hour or so. Then smile and go seek out your host. Introduce yourself and take a look at your room. Will you be using their sound system? How does it work? Is the microphone at a proper height? If it's a body mike, how does it attach? Is there a surface where you can put your books? What will you do with your handouts? You can put them on chairs, put a pile by the entry for people to pick up as they come in, or you can ask someone to hand them out.

Now go and get your books. I generally set my books up in the order I'm going to talk about them so that I can smoothly go from one to another. I keep handy a copy of the list of books that I'm booktalking, but it works better for me to cue off the books themselves. It's hard for me to focus on a list in the midst of a booktalk; it disrupts my concentration. I've been known to forget to talk about a book that wasn't available to me to bring but I put on the list anyway. Never fear, the audience will remind you.

Introductions

Introductions vary. Most service organizations will have a program chair that introduces you (from material that you've sent them). Many teachers give what Chance calls "the Superman introduction." Here's what he says about that particular phenomenon:

> The prologue to booktalking in the classroom often comes from the teacher or school librarian who introduces you as the local children's librarian who has come all the way from the public library to "talk about some really great books—now, pay attention!" This leaves you with the challenging task of describing books that students will want to know about, and in a way that will earn the level of attention that these students have been commanded to pay. You might as well been introduced as Superman, who will now run faster than a speeding locomotive. Do not despair. The great thing about booktalking to students is that you can become Superman, and you can leave that speeding locomotive in the dust."

Most community or book groups will simply introduce you with a few words about who you are and where you work. Be prepared, even if you are more formally introduced, to say a few words about yourself and what you're going to do. The audience needs a few moments to get used to you and your voice and settle in before they really start hearing you. I generally say something like, "Good morning. I'm delighted to be here. My name is Chapple Langemack, and I work for the King County Library System. I have the great good fortune of talking about books for a living. I brought some books with me this morning that I thought you'd enjoy. I try to talk about those undiscovered gems you may not have heard of rather than best-sellers, but mostly I talk about books I love. So let's start with . . ."

I've been to many a training session that recommends engaging your audience right off with a question. I like that idea a lot, and I've tried it a number of times. But it has never felt right to me. Perhaps I'm asking the wrong question. Give it a try and see if it works for you.

You're On

Breathe, relax, have fun. You have a boatload of great books to share with your audience. If you enjoy yourself, they will, too. Keep track of your time. I have a watch with really big numbers, so I don't have to work too hard to figure out what time it is. Many people like to take off their watch and put it on the podium. Those old school room clocks are the best. They are enormous, easy to read, and make a big clunking noise for each minute (or at least they used to). Digital clocks are just not the same.

Be flexible and don't worry about mistakes. Actor and comedian Robin Williams says someone once told him, "Mistakes are a Buddhist gift." You're audience is on your side, you love your books. It will all work out.

Dealing with Disruptions

Disruptions are going to happen at some point in time, so accept it as the price of doing business. Recently I spoke to a group of seniors at a YMCA in a room shared by seniors and teens. In mid presentation, a young woman entered from the rear, threaded her way through the audience, plunked herself down at a desk about three feet from where I was standing, and proceeded to boot up a computer with all the requisite electronic sound effects. Was any attention on me at the moment? Not one iota. I paused and looked, just as my audience did, looking, I'm sure, a little perplexed at this turn of events. When we all figured out what was going on I went back to my booktalks, cranking up the volume and energy levels to compensate.

And then there are the dreaded cell phones. If you suspect this may be a problem, you may wish to ask your audience to set their phones to vibrate before you begin. I loved the response of one presenter who, when an audience member's cell phone rang in the middle of her talk, called out, "If it's for me, tell them I'll call them back!" Mostly I identify with the chef at a very small *tapas* bar in Seattle. Cell phones are banned in his restaurant and should any customer display one, he stands over them menacingly with a very large, very sharp chef's knife. I've also seen him snatch up a customer's cell phone and make threatening motions toward the gas flames of the commercial range. I haven't resorted to brandishing knives at booktalks yet, but the day may come.

When all is said and done, the best that you can do with any kind of disruption is try to keep your focus. There will occasionally be backchat in the crowd or someone rooting around endlessly in a purse or backpack. Most of the time, your best course of action will be to ignore it and proceed as best you can. If the disruption is out of the ordinary—like a fire truck passing by, or in my instance, a computer interloper—you can acknowledge it nonverbally by pausing and waiting and then continuing, or you can acknowledge it verbally. Just last week I was speaking to a large group at a neighboring library system's all-staff meeting. Half way through the first book (you know, the smooth, polished corker that you start off with) I noticed a small hubbub, lots of muttering and twisting to and fro. I stopped talking and asked if there was a problem. It turned out not everyone had picked up a handout. So we solved that problem and I finished the book.

Half way through the second book, I noticed everyone's head cranked severely to the right. I looked over and saw the brightly outlined shadow of a window washer's squeegee moving up and down, up and down. I stopped dead and howled with laughter. What are the odds? We all giggled together for a minute. I said something to the effect of, "It may be window washing to him, but it's puppet theater to us," and my hostess kindly went out and requested that windows in a different part of the building be washed for awhile. Rare as this kind of occurrence is, it worked well to acknowledge it and move on. Everyone settled down, and we had a fine time for the rest of booktalk.

When you are booktalking in a school you may have a student who gives you trouble, so have some tricks up your sleeve for handling hecklers before a teacher has to interrupt to momentum of your booktalk to intervene. One classic schoolteacher trick is to move while you're talking and stand by the disruptive one. Carry on with your booktalk from there until the situation quiets.

Jeani says, "My most effective tool is to stop talking while in the middle of my booktalk if there is disruptive behavior going on. I also keep my eyes on the perpetrator, which means that the classmates who are listening watch the disruption, too."

I agree with Jeani about focusing on the perpetrator, another technique from the storyteller's bag of tricks. I use it with chatty adults as well. Keep on with your booktalk as normal but instead of making your eye contact around the room as you normally would, focus just on the one individual. It's okay to be intense about it; you really want them to be aware of your attention. In most instances, that's all it takes for the disruptive one to back off.

When I was regularly booktalking to young adults, I often included *Farewell to Manzanar* by Jeanne Watkasuki Houston. I love the book and think it's an important and compelling story, but I also used it to quell an obstreperous student if necessary. I opened the booktalk by choosing a student from the class and having him or her stand up. This is a great opportunity to put some heat on the smart mouth. "You know what?" I'd say to the student pretty sternly, "I don't like your looks. You have forty-eight hours to sell your house and get rid of all your belongings. Then I want you and all of your family to report to the train station at 8 A.M. You can each bring two suitcases, and that's it. Got it?" The focus, plus the thought of really having to do this generally subdued the troublemaker. I then went on with the booktalk, explaining that this is what really happened to Jeanne and her family during the Japanese internment.

Darcy is a beginning booktalker, and I enjoyed her comment: "There was a kid winking at me and making kissy faces from the back of the room during one presentation. I am still working on that poker face so I don't smile or laugh out loud . . . I think that one will take the most practice!"

Closing and Questions

After you're done talking about your books, prepare a sentence or two to close out your presentation and let your audience know you're finished. It need not be elaborate. For example, "That's what I've brought for you today. Thank you for being such a gracious audience. If you'd like to request any of the books I've mentioned today, you can call your local library or our Answer Line. That number is on your booklist. And you can log on to kcls.org at any time and look for more recommendations under 'Good Reads.' I'll leave you with the words of the great literary figure Groucho Marx who once said, 'Outside of a dog a book is man's best friend.' [long pause] 'Inside of a dog it's too dark to read.' Thanks for inviting me."

If you like (and have the time), you can offer to stay for a few minutes after the booktalk in case anyone wants to come up and look at the books. This won't work for service clubs on a tight luncheon deadline, but book groups and others often like to eyeball the books and chat informally with you about things they've read.

Many service organizations ask that you leave time for questions. Ten minutes or so is plenty. If you are speaking to adults, prepare yourself for the big pause that comes at the beginning of the question period. Rarely does anyone really have a burning question, but they want to be nice. The first question is what author Rick Bragg calls "the pity question." They feel sorry for you standing up there, waiting, so they ask something, anything. That breaks the ice, and more questions follow.

It's interesting that the questions I get from kids and from adults aren't really that different. Adults always want to know how many books I read. (My answer? Not nearly enough!) Kids will always ask, "Did you really read all those books?" Sometimes with service clubs, I get political or organizational questions ("How's that new library coming along?" or "Why don't we have a new library?"), so I try to keep current on the big picture of library activities. But most groups ask me questions about myself ("Where did you get the name Chapple?") or the books. Many want to recommend books they have read. It's not uncommon for someone to come up afterward to ask for recommendations, often relating to a son or daughter. Sometimes I can come up with something, but, as you know, it's hard to do without a catalog or collection in front of you. I never hesitate to have them call and talk to their local children's or young adult librarian, and I try to give them a specific name. "Mike is the young adult librarian at the Issaquah Library, and he's a whiz. I'd give him a call and see what he can recommend."

Pack Your Bags and Call It a Day

When you are truly through, thank your host for inviting you and pack up your gear. When you get back to your desk, make notes on what worked and what didn't. Note what you'd do differently if you talked to this group again. Put a booklist in your file so that you have a record. Also send a copy of the booklist to any other branches or departments that might be affected. When I speak at a senior residence, I send a list to the closest branch and to the staff of our Traveling Library Center who visit that facility. I also post it on our staff-only Intranet, so that anyone in the branches can check and see what I've been talking about lately.

A nice touch is to send a note to your host thanking him or her for inviting you—and enclosing a business card. It doesn't happen that often and makes you stand out. I've hosted many an author and presenter, and I'm thrilled when I get a note of thanks.

Now restock your essentials bag and put your books back in your booktalk collection. You did it! I knew you could.

It doesn't seem like it was so very long ago that Angelina Benedetti was a newly minted young adult librarian for whom I got to play crusty old librarian/mentor, giving advice on booktalking and young adult collection development and whatever else I thought she needed to know. Now Angie is an accomplished young adult librarian who can tell the rest of us a thing or two. Here's Angie's very clever and very true take on what it takes for a day of booktalking.

Angelina's Hierarchy of Needs

On occasion I am asked to speak to a legion of new, or soon-to-be-new, librarians on the fine art of booktalking. My own preparation in the craft was adequate but did not quite speak to the experience of standing in front of a real audience of teens. Like most newcomers to the field, I could have used a book such as this one to guide my way.

I have found many sources that speak to the construction of the booktalk itself. I have seen far fewer sources that speak to the experience of booktalking, of what to anticipate and prepare for in giving your talk. No two people will sell a book exactly the same way. Personal style dictates a talker's content, but the experience itself is remarkably similar from one circumstance to the other.

To organize my thinking, I began describing the experience of booktalking within the framework of Maslow's Hierarchy of Needs. In the 1960s, Abraham Maslow developed this hierarchy as a way of describing the human path from the meeting of biological needs to self-actualization. In his theory, physical needs must be met before security needs; security needs before social needs, and so on up the pyramid to self-fulfillment. Although I would not go so far as to adopt his theory wholesale, the compartmentalization of needs makes for a useful hanger on which to drape my own perceptions.

As mentioned, Maslow starts with the basics. Food, water, shelter, and oxygen are basic biological and physiological needs that must be met before moving to security needs. Except in times of social unrest, adults do not experience these needs as strongly as children do. When security needs have been met, we require love, affection, and belonging. Our ego must next be satisfied. We desire a high level of self-respect and hope for the respect of others. Finally, when all else has been achieved, we can look for self-actualization, a life outside of our own person where we capitalize on our gifts and talents for the benefit of the greater good.

Maslow's upwardly mobile model presumes movement from one plane to the next. I have found that in booktalking, as in so many other areas of librarianship, it is more accurate to say that we end up thinking about everything at once. I use Maslow's theory not as a prescription but as a way to organize my practical experience. So follows my Booktalker's Hierarchy of Needs, with apologies to Abraham Maslow.

Biological Needs

- No amount of preparation does as much as a good night's sleep.
- Always eat breakfast if you will be booktalking, a light one if you (like me) have a nervous stomach.
- Bring a water bottle.
- If you are going to be spending the day talking, find out where the bathroom is and if you will be getting a lunch break.
- Cafeteria food is less appealing to adults than to students. Consider bringing your own lunch, especially if you have special food needs.

Take a quick walk or do a yoga stretch during that lunch break. It will recharge you for the afternoon.

Dress in layers. School temperatures vary widely month to month, day to day, and class period to class period.

Security and Safety Needs

- Find out in advance where your host would like you to park and if a pass is required.

- Always check in at the school office or front desk. Many campuses now have security officers on site and you will need a visitor's pass.

- Some teachers have been known to use a booktalker's visit as an opportunity to visit the break room or run an errand. It is not a good or a safe thing to leave you, a visitor, as the sole adult in the classroom.

Love, Affection, and Belonging Needs

- Teens are teens, and you are not one of them. As an adult in their midst, do not try too hard to be liked. Being yourself, in all of your glory, will have a far greater impact.

- An engaged audience will not always look engaged.

- Keep classroom and teacher thank you notes in a special file. Pull that file out when you have had an experience lousy enough to make you want to quit your job and move to Italy. It happens to the very best of us, and the letters are a reminder that somebody, somewhere, loved what we did.

- Along these same lines, keep a picture of a loved one in your wallet. When things are not going well, take out that picture and look at it.

Ego and Esteem Needs

- When preparing your talk, think in terms of outcomes. What would you like to see happen at this talk? What do you hope the audience will take away? Articulating these outcomes helps you evaluate your success at the end in a more objective way than just saying, "Did I do well?"

- Track the circulation of the books you have just talked by creating a display, with multiple copies, when you return to the library. Your audience will know where to find them and you will know which titles were more or less of a draw.

- Mentally tally all of the different names your audiences create for you. I have a difficult name for students to swallow and so became "The Library Lady," "The Book Queen," "The Reading Goddess," "She-Who-Knows-Every-Book-There-Is," among others. Smile when they call you by these endearments back at the library.

Self-Actualization and Fulfillment

- Outcomes are great for a single performance, but ask yourself what you really hope to accomplish by booktalking, in a meta-sense. You may at some time need to defend the amount of time and energy you spend in this activity to your superiors and to yourself. Having internalized your reasons for engaging in this "higher calling," you will not be caught short when the question comes.

- Remind yourself that a relatively small percentage of the population volunteers to speak publicly and an almost miniscule percentage of that group could stand to do it in front of an audience of teens. You are saintly before you even open your mouth.

- Cherish the times when the energy is just right and the magic happens.

Additional Reading

📖 Kinsel, Brenda. *40 Over 40: 40 Things Every Woman Over 40 Needs to Know About Getting Dressed.* Berkeley, Calif.: Wildcat Canyon Press, 1999.

If you are "of a certain age" and go through periods when nothing in stores looks good—or even feasible—this upbeat book is for you.

📖 Kinsel, Brenda. *In the Dressing Room with Brenda: A Fun and Practical Guide to Buying Smart and Looking Great.* Berkeley, Calif.: Wildcat Canyon Press, 2001.

If you stress out every time you dress for an audience, this book will help calm your nerves.

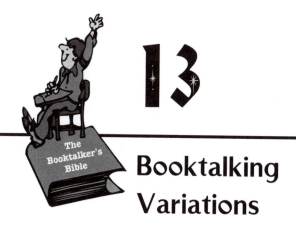

Booktalking Variations

Sometimes you need to talk to people about books in an engaging way, but a structured booktalk isn't appropriate or isn't all the information you need to give. This is the time to use your booktalk as a foundation and tinker with it so that it's appropriate for that particular circumstance.

Handselling

If you work in a public library, you've probably noticed that every patron who walks in the door thinks you've read every book in the library. It's truly magical the way that works. Think about it. Do you walk into a grocery store and expect every checker to be a gourmet cook? Or even recognize every piece of produce? Do you walk into the video store expecting a learned discourse from the pierced sixteen-year-old working there on the merits of Fellini versus Altman or even Barry Levinson versus Spike Lee? I don't think so.

But yet, for whatever reason, patrons walk into the library and want to hear about something good to read. And you have a lot of terrific books to tell them about. So I say, glory in it. Rejoice in it. Milk it for all it's worth. After all, how many times in this world do people really, truly want your opinion?

Use your time as you're walking (slowly!) over to the stacks to gather as much information as you can about what the patron is looking for. Have them tell you about books that they've enjoyed and listen to see if you can identify genres or pick up on appeal factors. Sometimes they don't really know themselves, and sometimes they are looking for books for someone

151

else, which is why they've come to you in the first place. They don't have a clue what their son or elderly mother would like to read—that's your job. Ain't it grand?

Our goal here is not to figure out which books to tell them about. That's the readers' advisory process, a topic that is several books unto itself. Remember Joyce Saricks, Nancy Pearl, and Duncan Smith? Instead, let's focus on how to compress your booktalk into a handsell, or shelf talk, a quick and informal introduction to the book.

As you're getting ready to talk about the books, consider Joyce Saricks's cautionary about using the word *recommend*. Saricks contends that when you recommend a book to a patron, you've set yourself up as the One Who Knows, making it uncomfortable for them to reject your recommendation. She considers "suggest" as a less emotionally charged word to use in this situation.

I always think of my friend Catherine's confession that as a child she would agonize over the stacks of books her local librarian would recommend to her. Too intimidated and embarrassed and just too darned nice to speak up and say that she didn't like them and didn't want them, she'd check them out and then return them several days later, unread.

But back to handselling. Most quick handsells have two components, the description and the evaluation, and both, clearly, are really brief. The description hearkens back to your booktalk hook—the part of the book that you found so appealing. Only now, standing at the shelf with a patron, you can't do the clever build up you'd do in a three-minute booktalk. Well, you could, but your patron would start to squirm, and you'd get some odd looks.

So pick out the part of the book that you found captivating, just as you did for your booktalk. Just like your booktalk, the "hook" for your handsell will be an appeal factor. It might be the premise, the setting, the character, the writing or the affect. Then condense the hook to one sentence. Here are some examples:

- Beryl is hired to photograph polar bears in Churchill, Manitoba, because she is small enough to fit inside the iron cage that will be placed on the ice among the bears. (*The Cage* by Audrey Schulman)

- The detective in *Trouble of Fools* is a six-foot-tall, red-headed, ex-cab driver named Carlotta. (*Trouble of Fools by Linda Barnes*)

- Monsieur Pamplemousse is a food critic who is ably assisted by his dog, a gourmand bloodhound named Pommes Frittes. (*Monsieur Pamplemousse* by Michael Bond)

- *A Free Man of Color* takes place during Mardi Gras in New Orleans in 1833. (*A Free Man of Color* by Barbara Hambly)

- Young, smart Mary Russell comes across an older man tending his hives on the Sussex Downs, who turns out to be Sherlock Holmes. (*The Beekeeper's Apprentice* by Laurie R. King)

Then build on your description with a sentence that conveys the mood, tone, or affect of the book. It's a one-two punch. Think truly descriptive. This is not the time to say, "I really liked this book" or "This is a wonderful book." That doesn't tell anybody anything except that you personally liked it. We want to know *why* you liked it. Think Johnny Carson: How small was it?

I was in a wine store recently looking for a wine to go with a special dinner. I asked an employee for a recommendation for something to go with a wild mushroom lasagne. Once we'd established a price range, he led me to a particular wine. He told me the region in Italy where it was from and the other kinds of wines it was related to. He made me promise to decant it two hours before I served it and assured me that it would "knock my socks off!" I purchased it, excited to have a great wine to complement my husband's fabulous homemade lasagne. I faithfully decanted it and prepared to be amazed by my first sip. I was underwhelmed. It wasn't a bad wine, certainly, but it didn't have me smacking my lips either. My socks were definitely still on.

Reflecting on this wine handsell, I wondered where it went wrong. He did a lot of things right. He established the price—which, I guess, has a parallel if you work in a bookstore. ("I'd like a book for the plane for under $15, please.") In the library that might correspond to the number of pages. ("I'd like a quick read for the beach this weekend." Or "My book report is due the day after tomorrow. I need a skinny book.")

He drew a parallel to other genres, telling me the other wines of the region (I'd like a mystery that's a police procedural."), and he gave me some cautionary advice about decanting ("This novel is a little slow to start, but if you stick it out, things really pick up in the fourth chapter.").

I realized that while he had sung the praises of the wine as one he really liked ("the best vintage of the century!"), he never gave me any clues to the characteristics of the wine itself. I didn't know going into it whether it would be dry, fruity, complex, full bodied, or what. And, I might add, I didn't ask, so propelled was I by the wine store guy's enthusiasm.

Just as we all have different tastes in food and drink, we all have different reading tastes. Even when we all drink the same wine or read the same book, our reactions are different based on our own preferences and life experiences. My wine guy's fabulous vintage was just an average bottle in my eyes—or rather on my palate.

So it's up to you to give your reader not only a sense of the plot, but also a sense of the tone or affect. Is it intense, suspenseful, light, richly detailed, spare, funny, quirky? You can even dip into wine adjectives: lush, plummy, fresh, tart, austere, juicy. You might want to compare it to something else your patron would know about.

Here are some examples:

📖 *Iron Lake* by William Kent Kruger; feels like Tony Hillerman meets the movie *Fargo.*

> This tells your patron, I hope, that the book is set in a cold northern clime and has some Native American folklore woven into the plot. Of course, you could just say, "This book is set in Minnesota and has a lot of Native American influence." But the description of Hillerman and *Fargo* is a little richer—it's shorthand that evokes lots of different images.

📖 *Fever Season* was so rich in historical detail, I could see, hear, and smell eighteenth-century New Orleans.

> This tells your patron where and when the book is set and that the setting is a strong factor in the book.

It's okay to interject your reaction to the book, after all your personal suggestion is part of what your patron is after. Just make sure to give them some clues with which to make their own decision.

- When I read *I Want to Buy a Vowel* by John Welter, I laughed so hard I snorted milk out my nose. It takes place in a small town in Texas that's full of characters.

- *The Cage* was so vivid, I nearly froze to death in August.

- I was really intrigued by the author's historical notes in *Pope Joan,* citing the evidence that suggests there really was a female Pope.

Okay? Got the drift? Let's put some together. You can time me if you want, I bet they are all under a minute.

- In *London Holiday,* three middle-aged ladies who were best of friends in high school vacation in London together. They go shopping, they have tea, they admire antiques, they go sightseeing, and there's a little romance in there, too. It's a quick read and the next best thing to a plane ticket.

- In *Pied Piper* by Ridley Pearson, detective Lou Boldt is trying to discover who is kidnapping children and leaving a penny flute in their crib. The situation becomes more desperate when his own daughter disappears. It's set in Seattle and is like J.A. Jance with more grit and sex.

- In Homer Hickam's memoir *Rocket Boys,* he and his friends, inspired by Sputnik, decide to build a rocket. The descriptions of the small West Virginia mining town that he lives in are so evocative, you feel like you're covered with coal dust when you finish.

- Rick Bragg tells the story of growing up poor in Alabama and eventually becoming a Pulitzer Prize–winning journalist. *All Over But the Shoutin'* is *Angela's Ashes* with a side of grits (or southern fried *Angela's Ashes*, I can't decide which).

Peer Booktalks

You may be called upon to booktalk to your colleagues, be it the librarians in your school district, the faculty in your building, or your fellow branch librarians. If you are presenting titles for them to read for their own enjoyment, then you'll do standard booktalks, giving them a snapshot of each book. If, however, you are talking about books that they might use with their students or patrons, you'll need to add some information.

Folks dealing with kids of any age are going to want to know the age-appropriateness of the title. Give some thought to not only the reading level of the text, but also the maturity level required to handle the content.

Teachers and school librarians are going to want to hear some ideas for curriculum use. They'll also want to be warned if there is sexual content, offensive language, or graphic violence. You don't need to express an opinion about the appropriateness of the book, just identify points that may be a concern. Most groups of librarians or other readers' advisors will want to know if the book is a particular genre or subgenre, and they'll be glad to know if you think it's a readalike for another author.

Sometimes a little extra can add the information called for to your booktalk. Here's an example.

📖 *Plain Truth* by Jodi Picoult

Hotshot Philadelphia defense attorney Ellie Hathaway desperately needed a break. She had just won yet another high-profile case, but she was tired of defending sleazeballs. She and her boyfriend seemed to have reached a stalemate in their relationship, and she wasn't sure where she wanted it to go. She just wanted to get away for a while and think about things. She decided to go to visit her aunt in rural Lancaster County. But instead of the rest, relaxation, and reflection she was looking for, she found herself coming to the defense of her cousin, a young Amish woman who had been accused of murdering her own baby. Ellie took on Sarah's defense, but it wasn't easy. Sarah not only proclaimed that she hadn't murdered her newborn, but that she had never even been pregnant.

If you have patrons who are fond of courtroom dramas that feature female protagonists, like Lisa Scottoline, have them try this one. *Plain Truth* by Jodi Picoult.

Media Talks

There are so many circumstances in which you could be talking about books on radio or television that it's difficult to give germane advice. If you are doing a cable show or your own radio spot, then it's pretty easy to format it just the way you want within your time limitations. It's when you're talking with someone about books on radio or television that it becomes difficult to give a standard booktalk. It's more like shelf talking or handselling to a patron. You can try to do your standard three-minute booktalk, but it's likely to look and feel odd.

When I was asked to do a recurring book segment on the local television morning news, I started off prepared to give my standard booktalk and quickly found that it didn't work at all in a three-minute segment shared with an anchor. My talk about the books had to be much more conversational in tone and much more impromptu. I never knew what comments or questions the host would have that I'd need to respond to. I finally found a method that worked. I picked out one appeal point, developed it into a sound bite, and took it from there with however much or little I could shoehorn in. These shows, and much of television, is geared toward people who are engaged in other tasks while the television is on, so a brief compelling point is about all anyone is interested in. For instance:

- Try to picture a one-armed guy in a rowboat going down the Grand Canyon with no map. (*Down the Great Unknown* by Edward Dolnick)
- Grace didn't want to hurt her boyfriend's feelings by breaking up with him, so she killed him instead. (*Nice* by Jen Sacks)

Cheesey it may be, but that's what worked for me. So be attentive and flexible, as you always are in booktalking, and you'll come up with a format that will suit the circumstances that you are working with. The great news is that you already did the hard part when you developed your booktalk. You know and can express the appeal of a book; all you have to do now is adapt that knowledge to a slightly different delivery. But you can do it. Once you've booktalked, you can master the universe. So go get 'em!

14

Evaluation and All That Jazz

You know how every time you go to a workshop, the organizers pass out a form at the end so you can evaluate the class you just took? They want to know if the learning objectives of the class were fulfilled. In other words, did you learn what you were supposed to? Those poor organizers. What they probably found out from the three evaluations they got back from the class of forty was that the room was too cold, the chairs were too hard, but the snacks at break were pretty good. Most people hate to fill out evaluations, me among them. That's why so many evaluation forms end up as handy pieces of paper for your grocery list. But, like it or not, evaluation is a job that most always has to be done, or at least considered. So let's get to it.

There are three areas to evaluate when you're booktalking. One is a personal skills evaluation—how you're doing as a booktalker. The second is evaluating the effectiveness of your booktalking program—is it doing what you thought? Are you reaching your intended audience? The third has to do with supporting the existence of your program. If the program is doing what you had in mind when you set out, then support should be easier to garner.

Evaluating Your Skills

Evaluating your booktalking skills is a personal thing. It's really up to you to gauge by the reaction of your audience if you were able to get your booktalks across and if you felt comfortable doing it. Your audience's reaction is probably going to tell you if the construction of your booktalk worked and if your phrasing and delivery was effective. It boils down to you and the audience and the energy and involvement you can feel in the room. As you do more and more booktalking, self-evaluation will become second nature to you. You'll note when you got a particularly good response to a particular hook, dramatic pause, or turn of phrase. You'll feel it when your energy is down and you haven't quite captured the room.

It's tempting to try and get feedback from your colleagues, but unless you are all on the same wavelength, that can be a dicey enterprise. Peer evaluation requires heaps of trust among the participants and needs to be carefully constructed so that you're getting only comments on observable behavior, not subjective opinions on whether you were any good. Feedback should be an observation of behavior coupled with a comment on what impact it had on the observer. "I had trouble hearing you from where I was sitting in the back of the room, and it made me feel left out" is legitimate. "You didn't engage my interest" is not. If you attempt peer evaluation, make sure your ground rules are set in advance and clearly understood.

Even videotaping is not the total answer. Watching yourself objectively on videotape (and who can do that, I want to know?) may tell you that you twiddle with your hair while you're talking or that you stare at the light fixture when you're trying to compose a thought. It may even get you to notice those ubiquitous "ums" or "you knows." That's certainly helpful information, but it's not the whole picture. A videotaped booktalk is a different medium from a live booktalk, just as watching videotape of a performance is much different from actually sitting in the theatre or symphony hall. You may see the façade of the presentation but don't get the personal connection, the essence of what went on. For most of us, watching a videotape of ourselves is just plain painful, and I'm not convinced what we get out of it is worth the trauma. But if you're made of sterner stuff, then videotape away and learn all you can.

Evaluating the Program

While evaluating your own performance is a personal issue, evaluating your booktalking program is another case altogether. Remember early on when I asked you to decide why you were booktalking in the first place? That's what you need to build on when you evaluate your program. What were you hoping to do? Were you after exposure for the library? Then it's meaningful that you spoke to twelve new groups. Were you trying to bring more kids in to the library? Then keep an eye on how speedily that display of books that you booktalked disappears or how quickly the holds queue builds on those titles. Keep track at the circulation and reference desk of the number of times staff hears "this lady (or guy) from the library came to my class.. . ." Maybe you'll want to give the kids a ticket that they can redeem for something (posters, magnets, pencils?) at the library and then tally your tickets. That would give you some data to work with.

Building Support

Much as we love to think that what we do as booktalkers is right, proper, virtuous, and noble, we'll still have to justify our existence from time to time. Here are some thoughts about how to do just that.

Do the Numbers

While you and I may agree that numbers don't always tell the whole story, see if you can't use them to support your program. Think of the facets of your booktalks that you can count—the number of presentations that you do, for one thing, and the number of people attending your booktalks for another. Are you turning down booktalks because you don't have time? Count those instances. You can count the number of times you have repeat customers or the number of times you've gotten a gig from referrals. You can track the circulation on the books you talk about, or watch for the number of holds on those titles. The thing is to look at the audience you were hoping to make contact with and look for evidence that you've reached them.

Take Testimony

Thank you notes are great to share with your supervisor. The fact that someone took the time to put pen to paper (or fingers to keyboard) in praise of your booktalking efforts carries weight with most administrators.

You can't really ask a booktalking audience to complete the kind of detailed evaluation that you'd ask for in a staff training session. It would be awkward to say the least. But you can ask for comments, and you can make it very easy. I periodically take our library's standard comment form with me when I go booktalking, especially to a new group. It's already addressed and ready to go. Then I say to an audience when I'm done, "My boss never gets to see what I do out here with you folks, so if you'd like to make a comment about some part of this program, please feel free. Here's a form that you can just fill out and send in."

We humans will invariably take the path of least resistance, so why not make it easy for your audience to comment on your booktalk? Create a self-addressed, stamped postcard like this one:

Thanks for inviting me to share some great books with you today. I'd appreciate your comments or suggestions for future presentations.

_____

_____

_____

_____

_____

_____

I suppose all this solicitation might be interpreted as shameless hucksterism. I prefer to think of it as striking while the iron is hot. If the members of your audience enjoyed your booktalks and like the fact that you're able to come to them, why not make it easy for them to say so? Do not underestimate the value of a handwritten phrase loving the fact that the library provides this wonderful service.

Closing Thoughts

Basically, the evaluation and justification of your booktalking program rests on the answers to two questions:

- How effectively you are accomplishing what you set out to do?
- How closely are your program objectives tied to the mission of the organization?

The mission of my own department is to "promote the value and pleasure of reading" to the adults in our service area. It's lucky for me that doing what brings me so much satisfaction is also an activity that matches that mission precisely. I hope that your own booktalking career brings you much joy in fulfilling your own goals.

Appendix A

Booktalk Titles

A

About the Author by John Colapinto
Cal Cunningham rockets to stardom with his first novel. There's only one problem—he didn't write it.

The Abracadabra Kid by Sid Fleischman
The autobiography of the Newbery award–winning children's author who set out from childhood to be a magician.

All Over but the Shoutin' by Rick Bragg
This Pulitzer Prize–winning journalist recounts his dirt-poor childhood in Alabama.

Amelia Earhart's Daughters by Leslie Haynsworth and David Toomey
The true story of women in aviation from World War II to the space program.

Animal Grossology: The Science of Creatures Gross and Disgusting by Sylvia Branzei
An icky concoction of real and memorable scientific facts, including how a fly eats, all about leeches, and the lowdown on bedbugs.

Anne Frank: The Diary of a Young Girl by Anne Frank
The autobiographical reminiscences of a young Jewish girl coming of age during World War II describes her life in hiding from the Nazis and offers a poignant study of the tragedy of the Holocaust.

As Long as She Needs Me by Nicholas Weinstock
Beleaguered Oliver Campbell is the personal assistant of the demanding Dawn of Dawn Books.

Attaboy, Sam! by Lois Lowry
Sam is able to help his sister Anastasia with the poem she is writing for their mother's birthday, but his own efforts to create a special perfume are disastrous.

Ava's Man by Rick Bragg
> In this sequel to *All Over but the Shoutin'*, Bragg tells the story of his mother's father.

B

Bald in the Land of Big Hair by Joni Rodgers
> Joni Rodgers' funny, gritty, poignant memoir of fighting (successfully!) non–Hodgkins lymphoma.

The Basket Counts by Arnold Adoff
> Illustrations and poetic text describe the movement and feel of basketball.

Bee Season by Myla Goldberg
> Extraordinary events are unleashed when Eliza Naumann, a seemingly unremarkable nine-year-old, suddenly displays a gift for spelling.

Beekeeper's Apprentice by Laurie R. King
> Tramping through the Sussex Downs, Mary Russell meets a retired beekeeper who turns out to be Sherlock Holmes.

Behind the Wheel by Janet Wong
> Thirty-six poems look at various aspects of driving, including passing the written driver's test and being pulled over by a cop.

Bel Canto by Ann Patchett
> A famous opera diva is hired to sing for a Japanese business titan in the home of a South American country's vice president.

Big Stone Gap by Adriana Trigiani
> Pharmacist Ave Maria Mulligan fancies herself the town spinster of Big Stone Gap, Virginia, leading a mundane and unexciting life in the wake of her mother's death. Then she discovers some skeletons in the family closet, and her whole world turns upside down.

Body Noises: *Where They Come From, Why Them Happen* by Susan Kovacs Buxbaum and Rita Golden Gelman.
> Here's the scoop of burps, snores, sneezes, cracking bones, and gas.

Bone (series) by Jeff Smith
> Excellent graphic novel for all ages, good adventure/fantasy tale.

The Bone Detectives: How Forensic Anthropologists Solve Crimes and Uncover Mysteries of the Dead by Donna M. Jackson
> Explores the world of forensic anthropology and its applications in solving crimes.

Bound Feet & Western Dress by Pang-Mei Natasha Chang

Intrigued by finding her family name in a Chinese history course, Natasha uncovers the astounding story of her great aunt.

Bowling Alone: The Collapse and Revival of American Community by Robert D. Putnam

Putnam shows how we have become increasingly disconnected from family, friends, neighbors, and our democratic structures and tells how we may reconnect.

Bug Faces by Darlene Murawski

Look deeply into the eight eyes of the nursery-web spider and see how you fare.

Buried in Ice: The Mystery of a Lost Arctic Expedition by Owen Beattie and John Geiger

Forensic anthropologist Beattie found (and photographed) the bodies of sailors on the 1845 Franklin expedition, a search for the Northwest Passage that came to a tragic end.

C

The Cage by Audrey Schulman

Beryl is hired to photograph Polar Bears in Churchill, Manitoba.

Call of the Wild by Jack London

A bold-spirited dog is stripped from his comfortable California estate and thrust into the rugged terrain of the Klondike in this allegorical adventure story demonstrating kindness amid the bitter cold and savage lawlessness of man and beast.

The Captain's Dog: *My Journey with the Lewis & Clark Tribe* by Roland Smith

Captain Meriwether Lewis's dog Seaman describes his experiences as he accompanies his master on the Lewis and Clark Expedition.

The Cat Who Went to Paris by Peter Gethers

Peter Gethers didn't want a cat, but when he received a Scottish Fold kitten as a gift, it was love at first purr.

Catcher in the Rye by J.D. Salinger

Holden Caulfield narrates the story of a couple of days in his sixteen-year-old life, just after he's been expelled from prep school.

The Catsitters by James Wolcott

When Johnny Downs comes home to his abandoned Manhattan apartment, he discovers that his cat sitter—also his girlfriend—has left more than his cat in the lurch.

A Chair for My Mother by Vera B. Williams
> A child, her waitress mother, and her grandmother save dimes to buy a comfortable armchair after all their furniture is lost in a fire.

The Chosen by Chaim Potok.
> The story of the friendship that develops between two Jewish boys in New York City.

CLICK, CLACK, MOO Cows That Type by Doreen Cronin
> Farmer Brown has a problem. His cows have found the old typewriter in the barn.

The Coalwood Way by Homer Hickam
> This sequel to Rocket Boys focuses on events in the town of Coalwood in 1959 while Homer and his friends are working on their rockets.

Cold Burial by Clive Powell-Williams
> In 1926, Edgar Christian and Jack Hornby were determined to demonstrate that civilized men could survive in the Barren Grounds of the Canadian Northwest Territories. They were wrong.

A Cold Day in Paradise by Steve Hamilton
> When two friends come to him for help, Alex McKnight, a former Detroit cop who runs a hunting camp on the shores of Lake Superior, investigates.

"The Colonel" by Carolyn Forche in *The Rag and Bone Shop of the Heart: Poems for Men* edited by Robert Bly, James Hillman, and Michael Meade.
> Poems in this collection are arranged by subject: war, wildness, loving the community.

A Complaint Is a Gift: Using Customer Feedback as a Strategic Tool by Janelle Barlow and Claus Moller.
> How to respond to feedback, especially when it isn't flattering or positive.

Cool Salsa: Bilingual Poems on Growing Up Latino in the United States edited by Lori M. Carlson.
> An assortment of poems that express Latino culture and the concerns of growing up in the United States.

Cool Women by Dawn Chipman, Mari Florence, and Naomi Wax (nonfiction)
> The thinking girl's guide to the hippest ladies in history, from Catwoman to Cleopatra.

Counterfeit Son by Elaine Marie Alphin
> When serial killer Hank Miller is killed in a shoot-out with police, his abused son Cameron adopts the identity of one of his father's victims to find a better life.

Courting Emma Howe by Margaret A. Robinson

> Emma is a Vermont spinster, buck toothed and plain. Arthur is a homesteader in Washington State, able but a might prickly. They've been corresponding for a long time.

Creepy Classics: Hair-Raising Horror from the Masters of the Macabre edited by Mary Hill

> Bram Stoker, Saki, Poe—they're all in here. Includes "The Monkey's Paw" by W.W. Jacobs.

D

A Darker Place by Laurie R. King

> Professor Anne Waverly infiltrates a suspicious religious cult.

Darkness Peering by Alice Blanchard

> Nalen Storrow is the police chief of Flowering Dogwood, Maine. The quiet life he had hoped for when he moved his family from the city is shattered when a young girl is found murdered.

The Devil's Teardrop by Jeffery Deaver

> It's New Year's Eve. A lone assassin, known only as The Digger, opens fire in a busy metro station in Washington, D.C. Later, a ransom note arrives at the mayor's office demanding $20 million by midnight.

Disgusting Digestion by Nick Arnold

> Answers burning questions such as, "How much pee can your bladder hold without popping?"

The Ditchdigger's Daughters: A Black Family's Astonishing Success Story by Yvonne S. Thornton, MD

> Donald Thornton, a ditchdigger in Monmouth, New Jersey, decided all five of his daughters would become doctors.

Dr. Jekyll and Mr. Hyde by Robert Louis Stevenson

> A kind and well-respected doctor can turn himself into a murderous madman by taking a secret drug he's created.

Don't Let's Go to the Dogs Tonight by Alexandra Fuller

> Curfews and war, mosquitoes, land mines, ambushes and "an abundance of leopards" are the stuff of Alexandra's childhood in Africa.

Down the Great Unknown by Edward Dolnick

> The story of the John Wesley Powell expedition down the Grand Canyon in 1869.

E

Earth-Shattering Poems edited by Liz Rosenberg
> A collection of poems that capture intense experiences and emotions by such authors as Sappho, John Keats, and, Emily Dickinson.

Earthshine by Theresa Nelson
> Slim watches over her father, a disarmingly charismatic man, as his struggle with AIDS reaches its climax.

The Eat-A-Bug Cookbook: 33 Ways to Cook Grasshoppers, Ants, Water Bugs, Spiders, Centipedes, and Their Kin by David George Gordon
> Recipes include Cockroach a la King and Bugs in a Rug.

Educating Esme by Esme Raji Codell
> This is Esme's first year teaching in inner-city Chicago.

The Elm at the Edge of the Earth by Robert D. Hale
> In the idyllically rural American Midwest, between the wars, young David is farmed out to relatives when his mother is hospitalized with a life-threatening illness.

The Endurance by Caroline Alexander
> Fabulous photos taken by Frank Hurley, the expedition's photographer, highlight this riveting tale of Ernest Shackleton's unsuccessful Antarctic expedition.

Ethel and Ernest: A True Story by Raymond Briggs
> The story of Briggs's parents' courtship and marriage, in graphic novel format.

Esperanza Rising by Pam Munoz Ryan
> Esperanza and her mother are forced to leave their life of wealth and privilege in Mexico to go work in the labor camps of Southern California.

F

The Face on the Milk Carton by Caroline Cooney
> A photograph of a missing girl on a milk carton leads Janie on a search for her real identity.

Fahrenheit 451 by Ray Bradbury
> In Bradbury's classic, frightening vision of the future, firemen don't put out fires, they start them to burn books.

Farewell to Manzanar by Jeanne Watkasuki Houston
> Jeanne and her family are interned after the Japanese bomb Pearl Harbor.

Fever Season by Barbara Hambly
>Benjamin January faces cholera and worse in this sequel to *A Free Man of Color*.

Five Sisters by Margaret Mahy
>Five paper dolls, all linked, go through a series of adventures hand in hand.

Fleur de Leigh's Life of Crime by Diane Leslie
>Growing up in Hollywood in the fifties, Fleur has a succession of unusual nannies.

Flowers for Algernon by Daniel Keyes
>Charlie Gordon, a retarded adult who cleans floors and toilets, becomes a genius through an experimental operation.

Foreign Exchange: A Mystery in Poems by Mel Glenn
>A series of poems reflect the thoughts of various people—town residents young and old, teachers, and some students visiting from the city—caught up in the events surrounding the murder of a beautiful high school student who had recently moved to the small lake-side community of Hudson Landing.

A Free Man of Color by Barbara Hambly
>Imagine New Orleans during Mardi Gras in 1833 through the eyes of Benjamin January, a free man of color.

Frindle by Andrew Clements
>When Nick is assigned an extra report for punishment, the results exceed anyone's expectations.

From the Bellybutton of the Moon and Other Poems by Francisco X. Alarcon
>A bilingual collection of poems in which the renowned Mexican American poet revisits and celebrates his childhood memories of summers, Mexico, and nature.

From Both Sides Now: The Poetry of the Vietnam War edited by Phillip Mahony
>Poetry by Americans in Vietnam as soldiers, Vietnamese children who lived through the war, and others who immigrated to the United States after the war.

G

Ginger Tree by Oswald Wynd
>At age twenty, Scotswoman Mary MacKenzie sets sail from Scotland to China to marry her military attaché fiancé and encounters a life she hadn't expected.

A Girl Named Zippy by Haven Kimmel
> A memoir of "growing up small" in Mooreland, Indiana, in the 1960s and 1970s.

Give a Boy a Gun by Todd Strasser
> Interweaves the voices of students, teachers, friends, and gunmen in a fictional story about two heavily armed students who hold their classmates hostage at a high school dance.

Good in Bed by Jennifer Weiner
> Publicly humiliated in her ex-boyfriend's magazine column, Candace Shapiro decides to make a few changes.

The Great Antler Auction by Susan Goodman
> A Boy Scout program in Jackson, Wyoming, collects elk antlers and sells them at auction to help pay for an elk feeding program at the National Elk Refuge.

Great Mambo Chicken and the Transhuman Condition: Science Slightly over the Edge by Edward Regis.
> The ideas and projects of scientists who are truly pushing the envelop.

The Greatest Generation by Tom Brokaw.
> The personal stories of those who fought World War II—at home and abroad.

Gross Grub: Wretched Recipes That Look Yucky but Taste Yummy by Cheryl Porter
> You have to have a strong stomach to even read these recipe titles: Boogers-on-a-stick, slab o' scabs, and veggie vomit.

Grossology Begins at Home: *The Science of Really Gross Things in Your Everyday Life* by Sylvia Branzei
> From toilets to toe jam—facts you really didn't want to know.

H

Homestead by Rosina Lippi
> A fictional account of the lives of women in a small Austrian village from 1909 to 1977.

Honus and Me by Dan Gutman
> Joey, who loves baseball but is not very good at it, finds a valuable 1909 Honus Wagner card and travels back in time to meet Honus.

The House on Mango Street by Sandra Cisneros
> Esperanza's childhood life in a Spanish-speaking area of Chicago is described in a series of spare, poignant, and powerful vignettes.

I

I Know What You Did Last Summer by Lois Duncan
> Four teenagers who have desperately tried to conceal their responsibility for a hit-and-run accident are pursued by a mystery figure seeking revenge.

I Know Why the Caged Bird Sings by Maya Angelou
> This memoir traces Maya Angelou's childhood in a small, rural community during the 1930s.

I Want to Buy a Vowel by John Welter
> Alfredo, an illegal alien from Guatemala, finds America much different than he anticipated.

I Will Be Cleopatra by Zoe Caldwell
> Acclaimed actress Caldwell recounts events in her life from her Australian childhood to her portrayal of Cleopatra (with Christopher Plummer as her Antony) in 1967.

In My Hands: Memories of a Holocaust Rescuer by Irene Gut Opdyke
> Recounts the experiences of the author who, as a young Polish girl, hid and saved Jews during the Holocaust.

The Invisible Man by H.G. Wells
> The eerie story of a mad scientist who makes himself disappear and goes murderously insane when he realizes that he cannot reverse the spell.

Into Thin Air by John Krakauer
> Krakauer's eyewitness account of what happened on a tragic Mt. Everest expedition.

Iron Lake by William Kent Krueger
> Part Irish, part Anishinaabe Indian, "Cork" O'Connor investigates some suspicious circumstances in Aurora, Minnesota.

Isaac's Storm by Erik Larson
> A riveting and detailed account of an extreme hurricane that killed eight thousand men, women, and children.

It's Disgusting—And We Ate It! True Food Facts From around The World—And Throughout History by James Solheim
> "It tastes like chicken!" Yeah, right.

It's Raining Pigs and Noodles by Jack Prelutsky
> Reciting "You Can't Make Me Eat That" may be just the segue you need to or from a gross book.

J

Joyful Noise: Poems for Two Voices by Paul Fleischman
>A collection of poems describing the characteristics and activities of a variety of insects.

Julie and Romeo by Jeanne Ray
>Romeo Cacciamani and Julie Roseman are rival florists in Boston whose families have hated each other for as long as anyone can remember. What they can't remember is why.

The Jump-Off Creek by Molly Gloss
>When her husband dies, Lydia Sanderson sells everything she owns and sets out to homestead in Oregon's Blue Mountains.

K

Kids Pick the Funniest Poems edited by Bruce Lansky
>Try "Willie the Burper" or "Could Have Been Worse" and you'll have an entire chorus of kids joining in with you.

L

La Cucina: A Novel of Rapture by Lily Prior
>When Rosa's lover is killed, she retreats first to the kitchen and then to Palermo.

Last Breath: Cautionary Tales from the Limits of Human Endurance by Peter Stark.
>In a fascinating blend of adventure and science, Stark recreates in heart-stopping detail what happens to our bodies and minds in the last moments of life when an extreme adventure goes awry.

The Last Days of Summer by Steve Kluger
>Twelve-year-old Joey takes desperate measures to catch the attention of famous third baseman Charlie Banks.

The Legend of Sleepy Hollow by Washington Irving
>A superstitious schoolmaster, in love with a wealthy farmer's daughter, has a terrifying encounter with a headless horseman.

Let the Celebrations Begin! by Margaret Wild
>Concentration camp survivors prepare for the liberation.

Letters from Yellowstone by Diane Smith
>In the spring of 1898, promising botanist A.E. Bartram is invited to join a field study in Yellowstone National Park.

A Life for a Life by Ernest Hill
> When his brother is held hostage by a drug dealer, D'Ray holds up a convenience store to get the money for his release.

The Lifted Veil: The Book of Fantastic Literature by Women, 1800—World War II edited by A. Susan Williams
> Includes the short story, "The Old Nurse's Tale" by Elizabeth Gaskell.

Light-Gathering Poems edited by Liz Rosenberg
> A collection of mostly classic poems that includes Dickinson, Yeats, Blake, Frost, and others.

Limbo by A. Manette Ansay
> From childhood, Ansay trained to become a concert pianist. But at nineteen, a mysterious muscle disorder forced her to give up the piano, and by twenty-one she couldn't grip a pen or walk across a room.

Little Lit: Folklore & Fairy Tale Funnies edited by Art Speigleman
> Innovative cartoonists and renowned children's book artists from around the world are contributors to this collection of stories ranging from old favorites to new discoveries.

Living Dangerously: Women Who Risked Their Lives for Adventure by Dorren Rappaport
> Six stories of American women who defied social convention to undertake dangerous adventures.

London Holiday by Richard Peck
> Three women find self-renewal, great shopping, and a little romance on a trip to London.

A Long Way from Chicago by Richard Peck
> Joey and his younger sister, Mary Alice, travel to visit their unconventional grandmother every August from 1929 through 1935.

Lucy Crocker 2.0 by Caroline Preston
> Lucy, a computer-clueless mom, becomes a most unlikely cyberspace superstar.

Lying Awake by Mark Salzman
> Sister John of the Cross must choose between her spiritual visions and her health.

M

Make Lemonade by Virginia Euwer Wolff
> To earn money for college, fourteen-year-old LaVaughn babysits for a teenage mother.

Man Eating Bugs: The Art and Science of Eating Insects by Peter Menzel
> I dare you to get past the cover photo—a young woman eating deep-fried tarantula on a skewer.

Maus: A Survivor's Tale: My Father Bleeds History by Art Speigleman

Maus II: A Survivor's Tale: And Here My Troubles Began by Art Speigleman
> The story of Vladek Speigelman, a Jewish survivor of Hitler's Europe, and his son, a cartoonist coming to terms with his father's story.

Meely LaBauve by Ken Wells
> While his Daddy's hunting gators, fifteen-year-old Meely mostly looks after himself. He does fine until nasty Junior Guidry torments him beyond bearing.

Meeting Luciano by Anna Esaki-Smith
> Emily has just graduated from college and is staying with her mother temporarily. Her mother, Hanako, announces that she's invited Luciano Pavarotti to the house.

Memories of a Lost Egypt by Colette Rossant
> Colette spends her growing up years with her Egyptian grandparents in a Belle Epoch mansion on the Nile in pre–World War II Cairo.

Metamorphosis by Franz Kafka
> A man finds himself transformed into a huge insect.

Mind's Eye by Paul Fleischman
> Unlikely nursing home roommates, sixteen-year-old Courtney and eighty-eight-year-old Elva take an imaginary journey together using a 1910 Baedeker's Guide to Italy.

Miss Garnet's Angel by Salley Vickers
> After the death of her longtime companion and roommate, retired schoolteacher Julia Garnet decides to spend six months in Venice.

Miss Julia Speaks Her Mind by Ann B. Ross
> Miss Julia Springer, longtime church member and pillar of the community, has recently buried her likewise estimable husband, Wesley Lloyd Springer. But Wesley has left something unexpected behind.

Missing May by Cynthia Rylant
> After being passed among relatives, Summer joins her aunt and uncle and marvels at the couple's deep love for one another.

"The Monkey's Paw" by W.W. Jacobs from *Creepy Classics: Hair-Raising Horror from the Masters of the Macabre* edited by Mary Hill
> Bram Stoker, Saki, Poe—they're all in here.

Motel of the Mysteries by David Macaulay
> What will a future people think when they unearth the remains of our civilization?

Monsieur Pamplemousse by Michael Bond
> Gourmand Monsieur Pamplemousse investigates, with the help of his discriminating dog, Pommes Frites.

Mountain City by Gregory Martin
> A poignant snapshot of a small mountain town in the Basque country of Nevada.

My Little Sister Ate One Hare by Bill Grossman.
> A vastly entertaining counting book. It will make you think of the old woman who swallowed the fly—only grosser!

My Many Colored Days by Dr. Seuss
> This rhyming story describes each day in terms of a particular color, which in turn is associated with specific emotions. One young adult librarian uses this one very successfully with middle school students.

N

Nice by Jen Sacks
> Grace is just too nice to break up with her boyfriend, so she kills him instead.

Night Garden: Poems from the World of Dreams by Janet Wong
> A collection of poems describing a variety of dreams, some familiar, some strange, some beautiful, and some on the darker side.

Nine Parts of Desire: The Hidden World of Islamic Women by Geraldine Brooks.
> An absorbing account of the lives of women in Islamic countries.

O

Of Mice and Men by John Steinbeck
> The tragic tale of a retarded man and the friend who loves and tries to protect him.

Oh Yuck! The Encyclopedia of Everything Nasty by Joy Masoff.
> From acne to maggots to vomit, it's in here.

"The Old Nurse's Story" by Elizabeth Gaskell in *The Lifted Veil: The Book of Fantastic Literature by Women, 1800—World War II* edited by A. Susan Williams.
> Includes work by Alcott, Stowe, and Karen Blixen, among others.

The Oldest Rookie: Big-League Dreams from A Small-Town Guy by Jim Morris
> Jim Morris was a high school physics teacher until becoming a professional ball player at age thirty-five.

Olivia by Ian Falconer
> Olivia the pig is good at singing forty very loud songs and is especially good at wearing people out.

One Flew over the Cuckoo's Nest by Ken Kesey
> An inmate of a mental institution tries to find the freedom and independence denied him in the outside world.

Out of the Dust by Karen Hesse
> In a series of poems, fifteen-year-old Billie Jo relates the hardships of living on her family's wheat farm in Oklahoma during the dust bowl years of the Depression.

P

Patrick Doyle Is Full of Blarney by Jennifer Armstrong
> In the summer of 1915, Patrick and his friends must fend off a rough gang who want to take over their Hell's Kitchen baseball diamond.

Peace Like a River by Leif Enger
> Ruben, his sister Swede, and his father undertake an unlikely Odyssey.

Pedro and Me: Friendship, Loss and What I Learned by Judd Winick
> In graphic art format, this book describes the friendship between two roommates on the MTV show *Real World,* one of whom died of AIDS.

The Perfect Elizabeth Libby Schmais
> As sisters Eliza and Bette grabble with men, parents, and jobs, Eliza wonders if together they wouldn't be a perfect whole.

The Persian Pickle Club by Sandra Dallas
> The ladies of Harveyville, Kansas, find solace in their quilting society during the dust bowl years.

Pied Piper by Ridley Pearson.
> Seattle Homicide detective Lou Boldt is called in to investigate the wave of babynappings that have swept the west coast.

Pierced by a Ray of the Sun: Poems About the Times We Feel Alone selected by Ruth Gordon
> An international anthology of poems about loneliness.

Plain Truth by Jodi Picoult

> Ellie Hathaway, a big time Philadelphia defense attorney retreats to rural Lancaster County hoping for a respite from her hectic life. Instead, she winds up defending a young Amish woman.

Poetry in Motion: 100 Poems from the Subways and Buses edited by Molly Peacock, Elise Paschen, and Neil Neches.

> A gathering of poetry on placards displayed in the subways and buses of New York City, ranging from Sappho to Sylvia Plath, from W.H. Auden to the ninth-century Chinese poet Chu Chen Po.

Pope Joan by Donna Woolfolk Cross

> Was there really a female Pope in the ninth century?

The Pumpkin Rollers by Elmer Kelton

> After the Civil War, young Trey heads west to find his future.

R

The Rag and Bone Shop of the Heart: Poems for Men edited by Robert Bly, James Hillman, and Michael Meade.

> Poems in this collection are arranged by subject: war, wildness, loving the community. Includes "The Colonel" by Carolyn Forche.

The Rat: A Perverse Miscellany collected by Barbara Hodgson

> A quirky compendium of rat facts, rat fiction, rat lore, and rat art.

Rats by Paul Zindel

> When mutant rats threaten to take over Staten Island, which has become a huge landfill, fourteen-year-old Sarah and her younger brother Mike try to figure out how to stop them.

Rescue Josh McGuire by Ben Mikaelsen

> When thirteen-year-old Josh runs away to the mountains of Montana with an orphaned bear cub destined for laboratory testing, they both must fight for their lives in a sudden snowstorm.

Roald Dahl's Revolting Rhymes by Roald Dahl

> Humorous retellings of six well-known fairy tales featuring surprise endings in place of the traditional happily ever after.

Rocket Boys: A Memoir by Homer Hickam

> Looking back after a distinguished NASA career, Hickam shares the story of his youth in a coal-mining town. The movie *October Sky* was based on this book.

The Rose That Grew from Concrete by Tupac Shakur

> A collection of more than one hundred poems that confront topics ranging from poverty and motherhood to Van Gogh.

The Run by Stuart Woods
>Senator Will Lee decides to run for president when he learns that the current vice president has Alzheimer's disease.

S

Save Queen of Sheba by Louise Moeri
>After their wagon train is attacked by Indians, King David must try to save himself and his sister, Queen of Sheba.

The Scary Story Reader: Forty-One of the Scariest Stories for Sleepovers, Campfires, Car & Bus Trips—Even for First Dates by Richard Young and Judy Dockrey Young
>A collection of scary urban legends and other modern-day horror tales.

Seabiscuit: An American Legend by Laura Hillenbrand
>The true story of a remarkable horse.

The Secret House: 24 Hours in the Strange and Unexpected World in Which We Spend Our Nights and Days by David Bodanis
>There's a lot going on in your house that you neither see nor know about.

A Separate Peace by John Knowles
>Knowles's classic story of two friends at boarding school during World War II.

Slam edited by Cecily Von Ziegesar
>This is teen poetry, side by side with the rants of the Beat poets, the verses of Shakespeare, and the rhymes of hip-hop. Also included is an explanation of poetry slams and writing tips for budding poets.

Slow Dance Heart Break Blues by Arnold Adoff
>Poetry describing—and revealing—the ups and downs of the young adult's struggle to define self.

Sol a Sol: Bilingual Poems written and selected by Lori M. Carlson
>A collection of poems by various Hispanic American writers that celebrate a full day of family activities.

Space: A Memoir by Jesse Lee Kercheval
>Jesse Lee's family moves to Florida just as the preparation for the moonshot is in full swing.

Speak by Laurie Halse Anderson
>A traumatic event near the end of the summer has a devastating effect of Melinda's freshman year in high school.

Stick Figure by Lori Gottlieb
> An eleven-year-old's diary of anorexia.

Stone Bench in an Empty Park: Haiku edited by Paul Janeczko
> An anthology of haiku accompanied by photographs reflects nature in the city.

Stop Pretending: What Happened When My Big Sister Went Crazy by Sonya Sones
> A younger sister has a difficult time adjusting to life after her older sister has a mental breakdown.

Stopping by Woods on a Snowy Evening by Robert Frost, illustrated by Susan Jeffers
> A beautifully illustrated rendition of this Frost poem.

The Story of Z by Jeanne Modesitt
> Tired of being the last in line and feeling unappreciated, Z walks off the alphabet and decides to start her own.

A Suitcase Full of Seaweed and Other Poems by Janet Wong
> Wong reflects on her Korean and Chinese heritage in these poems.

Swallowing Stones by Joyce McDonald
> During Michael's seventeenth birthday celebration, he discharges an antique Winchester rifle and unknowingly kills the father of a high school classmate.

The Sweet Potato Queens' Book of Love by Jill Conner Brown
> The Sweet Potato Queens are legendary in Jackson, Mississippi, and they'll give you all the advice you need—and then some.

Sylvester and the Magic Pebble by William Steig
> In a moment of fright, Sylvester the donkey asks his magic pebble to turn him into a rock but then cannot hold the pebble to wish himself back to normal again

T

Taking Lottie Home by Terry Kay
> It's 1904. Foster Lanier and Ben Phelps have just been cut from their Georgia baseball team and are headed home on the train. Then they meet Lottie.

The Tale of One Bad Rat by Bryan Talbot
> The tale of an abused girl obsessed with Beatrix Potter who goes on a journey across England to confront her personal demons.

Talking Like the Rain: A Read to Me Book of Poems by X.J. Kennedy
 An illustrated collection of poems for very young children, including works by Robert Louis Stevenson, Edward Lear, Shel Silverstein, and Jack Prelutsky.

Teen.com Book of Poetry edited by Missy Rekos
 Poems of love, family, friendship, and life written by teens from around the world.

Tender at the Bone by Ruth Reichl
 A restaurant critic and food editor's delicious memoirs.

Things I Have to Tell You: Poems and Writing by Teenage Girls edited by Betsy Franco
 A collection of poems, stories, and essays written by girls aged twelve to eighteen that speak about body image, seduction and betrayal, courage and failure, shame and pride.

A Time for Andrew: A Ghost Story by Mary Downing Hahn
 When he goes to spend the summer with his great-aunt in the family's old house, eleven-year-old Drew is drawn eighty years into the past to trade places with his great-great-uncle.

Time Stops for No Mouse by Michael Hoeye
 Adventures ensue when watchmaker mouse Hermux Tantamoq meets dashing aviatrix Linka Perfliger.

The Tipping Point by Malcolm Gladwell
 The theory of why trends happen or "social epidemics."

To Kill a Mockingbird by Harper Lee
 Through the young eyes of Scout and Jem Finch, Harper Lee explores with rich humor and unswerving honesty the irrationality of adult attitudes toward race and class in the Deep South of the 1930s when a black man is charged with the rape of a white girl.

Train Go, Sorry by Leah Hager Cohen
 One year in the life of New York City's Lexington School for the Deaf.

A Trouble of Fools by Linda Barnes
 Ex-cop Carlotta Carlyle dusts off her private investigator's license when an old woman asks her to find her missing brother—and a missing $13,000.

U

Under the Beetle's Cellar by Mary Willis Walker
 Eleven children and their school bus driver have been kidnapped by a religious cult and are being kept captive underground.

Uphill Walkers by Madeleine Blais
> In 1952, Madeleine's father dies suddenly, leaving behind a pregnant wife and five young children.

V

Vertical Run by Joseph R. Garber
> It's just another day at the office for Dave, until his boss tries to kill him.

A Visit to William Blake's Inn: Poems for Innocent and Experienced Travelers by Nancy Willard
> A collection of poems describing the curious menagerie of guests who arrive at William Blake's inn.

Voyage of a Summer Sun by Robin Cody
> Cody paddles the Columbia River from source to mouth.

W

Wait Till Next Year by Doris Kearns Goodwin
> A noted historian's memoir of growing up in the baseball crazed New York of the 1950s.

Walking Across Egypt by Clyde Edgerton
> Independent Mattie Rigsby, aged seventy-eight, finds an adolescent delinquent on her doorstep one day and takes unexpected action.

Whale Talk by Chris Crutcher
> TJ, a multiracial teenager, shuns organized sports and the gung-ho athletes at his high school until he agrees to form a swimming team and recruits some of the school's less popular students.

When the Rain Sings: Poems by Young Native Americans
> A collection of poems written by young Native Americans, inspired by or matched with photographs of artifacts and people from the National Museum of the American Indian.

Where the Sidewalk Ends by Shel Silverstein
> It's been around for a long time, but it's still a favorite. After all, who can resist a poem titled "Dancing Pants"?

Who Killed Mr. Chippendale? by Mel Glenn
> Free verse poems describe the reactions of students, colleagues, and others when a high school teacher is shot and killed as the school day begins.

Why We Buy: The Science of Shopping by Paco Underhill.
> Underhill can tell you just about anything you want to know about retailing.

Wild Life by Molly Gloss
> Charlotte joins the search for her housekeeper's missing granddaughter and gets lost herself.

Windfall by James Magnuson
> While searching for the family cat, Ben Lindberg finds eight coolers full of $500 bills in the basement of an abandoned building.

Winterdance by Gary Paulsen
> Paulsen recounts his trials and tribulations training for, and participating in, the Iditarod.

Woodsong by Gary Paulsen
> For a rugged outdoor man and his family, life in northern Minnesota is a wild experience involving wolves, deer, and the sled dogs that make their way of life possible.

The Worst Case Scenario Survival Handbook: Travel by Joshua Piven and David Borgenicht.
> Help for the perils of travel—from UFO abductions to volcanic eruptions.

Y

Year of Miss Agnes by Kirkpatrick Hill
> Ten-year-old Fred (short for Frederika) narrates the story of school and village life among the Athapascans in Alaska during 1948 when Miss Agnes arrived as the new teacher.

Year of Wonders by Geraldine Brooks
> Beset by the plague in the seventeenth century, an English village quarantines itself so as not to infect neighboring towns.

Yikes! Your Body Up Close! by Mike Janulewicz
> A book of microphotography of bodyscapes that look like alien planets. Yikes, indeed.

You Hear Me? Poems and Writing by Teenage Boys edited by Betsy Franco
> An anthology of stories, poems, and essays by adolescent boys on love, anger, sex, "monster" drugs, family, conformity, and being gay.

Yuck! A Big Book of Little Horrors by Robert Sneddon
> You may never eat toast again after looking at it 35,000 times normal size.

Z

Zipping, Zapping, Zooming Bats by Ann Earle
> Provides basic facts about the behavior of bats and describes how they benefit the environment.

Zoya's Story by Zoya with John Follain and Rita Cristofari.
> The story of an Afghan woman's struggle for freedom.

Appendix B

Additional Reading Lists

Additional Information on Booktalking Techniques

Bodart, Joni. *Booktalk! 2: Booktalking for All Ages and Audiences*, second edition. New York: H.W. Wilson, 1985.

> Advice on how to write and deliver a booktalk plus sample booktalks.

Bromann, Jennifer. *Booktalking That Works*. New York: Neal-Schuman Publishers, 2001.

> Information about booktalking methods and sample booktalks.

Jones, Patrick. *Connecting Young Adults and Libraries: A How to Do It Manual*, second edition. New York: Neal-Schuman, 1998.

> Patrick clearly lays out the mechanics of booktalking in the chapter "Booktalking: Don't Tell, Sell."

MacDonald, Margaret Read. *The Storyteller's Start-up Book: Finding, Learning, Performing and Using Folktales*. Little Rock, Ark.: August House, 1993.

> Check out the chapter "Learning the Story in One Hour" for techniques on remembering your booktalk.

Rochman, Hazel. *Tales of Love and Terror: Booktalking the Classics, Old and New*. Chicago: American Library Association, 1987.

> Good advice on building your booktalks. Particularly helpful on figuring out how to approach your book and how to choose passages to read aloud.

Help on Presentation Techniques

Kahle, Peter V.T., and Melanie Workhoven. *Naked at the Podium: The Writer's Guide to Successful Readings*. Seattle, Wash.: 74th Street Productions, 2001.

> A book for writers on tour promoting their own book, this volume has lots of helpful presentation hints for booktalkers as well.

183

Linklater, Kristin. *Freeing the Natural Voice*, 1976.
> One of the classic books on voice and breath, filled with lots of relaxation and focusing exercises.

Lipman, Doug. *Improving Your Storytelling: Beyond the Basics for All Who Tell Stories in Work or Play*. Little Rock, Ark.: August House, 1999.
> Good advice that booktalkers as well as storytellers can use on how to learn a story, use your voice well, and overcome fear.

Ristad, Eloise. *A Soprano on Her Head: Right-Side-Up Reflections of Life and Other Performances*. Moab, Utah: Real People Press, 1982.
> A wonderful blend of philosophy and pragmatism that will help you make your own rules for performing and for overcoming stage fright.

MacDonald, Margaret Read. *The Storyteller's Start-Up Book: Finding, Learning, Performing, and Using Folktales Including Twelve Tellable Tales*. Little Rock, Ark.: August House, 1993.
> You'll find the chapter "Performing the Story" to be applicable to booktalks as well.

Slutsky, Jeff, and Michael Aun. *The Toastmasters International Guide to Successful Speaking: Overcoming Your Fears, Winning Over Your Audience, Building Your Business and Career*. Chicago: Dearborn Financial, 1997..
> Take a look at the chapter "Developing Your Gestures, Body Language, Voice Modulation, and Vocal Variety."

Sources for Sample Booktalks

Baxter. Kathleen A., and Marcia Agness Kochell. *Gotcha! Nonfiction Booktalks to Get Kids Excited About Reading*. Englewood, Colo.: Libraries Unlimited, 1999.
> Lots of suggestions here for topics and specific nonfiction titles to use with elementary and middle school students.

Baxter. Kathleen A., and Marcia Agness Kochell. *Gotcha Again!* Englewood, Colo.: Libraries Unlimited, 2002.
> Even more suggestions of nonfiction titles to use with students.

Bodart-Talbot, Joni, editor. *Booktalk! 3: More Booktalks for All ages and Audiences*. New York: H.W. Wilson, 1988.
> Booktalks for all ages with helpful indexes for theme/subject, author/title, and age.

Bodart, Joni Richards, editor. *Booktalk! 4: Selections from "The Booktalker" for All Ages and Audiences*. New York: H.W. Wilson, 1992.
> Booktalks for all ages with helpful indexes for theme/subject, author/title, and age.

Bodart, Joni, editor. *Booktalk! 5: More Selections from "The Booktalker" for All Ages and Audiences*. New York: H.W. Wilson, 1993.

    More booktalks to look at here with some essays on booktalking experiences at the beginning of the book.

Bodart, Joni Richards, editor. *The Booktalkers' Companion: Volume I*. Denver, Colo.: BookHooks, 1994.

    Booktalks plus a great article on the ABCs of booktalking by Patrick Jones.

Bodart, Joni, editor. *The Booktalker*, *volume 2*. Denver, Colo.: Bookhooks, 1996.

Bromann, Jennifer. *Booktalking That Works*. New York: Neal-Schuman, 2001.

    Features research about teen reading interests plus information of booktalking methods and sample booktalks.

Littlejohn, Carol. *Keep Talking That Book!: Booktalks to Promote Reading, Volume II*. Worthington, Ohio: Linworth, 2000.

    Brief booktalks on a wide range of books "for ages 8 to 80" arranged in order by author.

Schall, Lucy. *Booktalks Plus: Motivating Teens to Read*. Englewood, Colo.: Libraries Unlimited, 2001.

    Booktalks grouped in topics relating to curriculum and to adolescent developmental tasks. Includes a summary of the book and related activities.

Ideas for Titles to Booktalk to Adults

Craughwell, Thomas. *Great Books for Every Book Lover: 2002 Great Reading Suggestions for the Discriminating Bibliophile*. New York: Black Dog & Leventhal, 1998.

    This is a great book to browse when you're looking for booktalk candidates. It's divided into categories that range from "Women of Substance" to "Great Gossip."

Herald, Diana Tixier. *Genreflecting: A Guide to Reading Interests in Genre Fiction*, fifth edition. Englewood, Colo.: Libraries Unlimited, 2000.

    This is a great one to help you find good reads in every genre.

Pearl, Nancy with assistance from Martha Knappe and Chris Higashi. *Now Read This: A Guide to Mainstream Fiction, 1978–1998*. Englewood, Colo.: Libraries Unlimited, 1999.

    A listing of literary fiction and their readalikes grouped by appeal factors.

Saricks, Joyce G. *The Readers' Advisory Guide to Genre Fiction.* Chicago: American Library Association, 2001.

> Fifteen major genres are covered here with the characteristics of the genre, key authors noted and "sure bets" for each genre that consistently appeal to a wide variety of readers.

Finding Great Titles to Booktalk to Children and Teens

Carter, Betty. *Best Books for Young Adults: The History, the Selections, the Romance.* Chicago: American Library Association, 1994.

> Good information of the history of ALA's Best Books for Young Adults, plus a gold mine of potential booktalking titles for teens from BBYA lists through the years.

Odean, Kathleen. *Great Books About Things Kids Love: More Than 750 Recommended Books for Children 3 to 14.* New York: Ballantine, 2001.

> Good browsing for nonfiction booktalk titles from baseball to cowboys to poetry plus lots and lots of critters.

Rochman, Hazel. *Tales of Love and Terror: Booktalking the Classics, Old and New.* Chicago: American Library Association, 1987.

> Good advice on building your booktalks. Particularly helpful on figuring out how to approach your book and how to choose passages to read aloud.

Rothschild, D. Aviva. *Graphic Novels: A Bibliographic Guide to Book-Length Comics.* Englewood, Colo.: Libraries Unlimited, 1995.

> Includes an in-depth explanation of what graphics novels are and an annotated bibliography of graphic novels by genre.

Schall, Lucy. *Booktalks Plus: Motivating Teens to Read.* Englewood, Colo.: Libraries Unlimited, 2001.

> Booktalks grouped in topics relating to curriculum and to adolescent developmental tasks. Includes a summary of the book and related activities.

Weiner, Stephen. "Beyond Superheroes: comics get serious." *Library Journal.* (February 1, 2002), p. 55.

> A good, brief introduction to graphic novels.

For Information on Child Development

Brownlee, Shannon. "Inside the Teen Brain" *U.S. News & World Report* (August 9, 1999), p. 44.

> The latest on teen brain research.

Gopnik, Alison, Andrew N. Meltzoff, and Patricia K. Kuhl. *The Scientist in the Crib: What Early Learning Tells Us About the Mind.* New York: Harper Trade, 2000.

Good information on child development issues.

When You Want to Know More About Doing Readers' Advisory

Saricks, Joyce G., and Nancy Brown. *Readers' Advisory Service in the Public Library*, 1997. Chicago: American Library Association, 1997.

This is the book to pick up if you want more information on appeal factors and how to conduct a readers' advisory interview.

Shearer, Kenneth D. *The Readers' Advisor's Companion.* Englewood, Colo.: Libraries Unlimited, 2001.

Essays on readers' advisory, from the philosophical to the pragmatic.

Saricks, Joyce G. *The Readers' Advisory Guide to Genre Fiction.* Chicago: American Library Association, 2001.

Fifteen major genres are covered here with the characteristics of the genre, key authors noted, and "sure bets" for each genre that consistently appeal to a wide variety of readers.

More Information on Book Group Mechanics and Recommended Reading

Jacobsohn, Rachel W. *The Reading Group Handbook: Everything You Need to Know to Start Your Own Book Club,* revised edition. New York: Hyperion, 1998.

This is probably the standard work on organizing and operating reading groups. There are lots of lists of suggested book group reading as well.

Paz & Associates. *Reading Group Choices: Selections for Lively Book Discussions.* Nashville, Tenn.: Paz & Associates, 2000, 2001, 2002.

Titles, summaries, brief author biographies, and sample discussion questions. Includes Internet addresses for additional information when available.

McMains, Victoria Golden. *The Readers' Choice: 200 Book Club Favorites.* New York: HarperCollins, 2000.

Tips about how to form and operate a book group are in front followed by a listing of books with a discussion of what their appeal is for book groups and a sample discussion question.

Slezak, Ellen. *The Book Group Book: A Thoughtful Guide to Forming and Enjoying a Stimulating Book Discussion Group,* second edition. Chicago: Chicago Review Press, 1995.

>An anthology of essays by book group members about the mechanics of a book group. There are lots of reading lists from book clubs all over the country.

When You Just Don't Know What to Wear

Kinsel, Brenda. *40 Over 40: 40 Things Every Woman Over 40 Needs to Know About Getting Dressed.* Berkeley, Calif: Wildcat Canyon Press, 1999.

>If you are "of a certain age" and go through periods when nothing in stores looks good—or even feasible—this upbeat book is for you.

Kinsel, Brenda. 2001. *In the Dressing Room with Brenda: A Fun and Practical Fuide to Buying Smart and Looking Great.* Berkeley, Calif.: Wildcat Canyon Press

>If you stress out every time you dress for an audience, this book will help calm your nerves.

Index

About the Author

In her twenty-something career as a public librarian, Chapple Langemack has done everything from nursing home visits to pre-school storytimes, not to mention toilets and windows. She is currently the Readers' Services Coordinator for the King County Library System near Seattle where, in addition to booktalking, she develops Web content, literary programming, and readers' advisory tools and training for staff.

Photograph by Nancy Clendaniel

In demand as a booktalker and a speaker on readers' advisory topics, she has spoken to readers, writers, teachers, and librarians at the local, state, and national levels including the American Library Association (ALA) and the National Council of Teachers of English. She has also taught at the University of Washington School of Library and Information Science.

Not content with trying to read herself blind as a member of the ALA's Best Books for Young Adults, she went on to serve on the organization's Notable Books Council, a group charged with choosing the year's top twenty-five books for adults. Her optometrist has officially disowned her.

In her non-reading, non-booktalking time, Chapple is a theatre devotee whose most memorable role involved removing and donning pantyhose on stage. She lives with the world's most amiable husband on Bainbridge Island in Washington State.

To hear Chapple read her booktalk of the month, visit
http://www.kcls.org/gr/bkmonth.cfm